Sacred F
of
The Lake District

A Handbook for Holiday Pilgrims

THE AUTHOR

W R (Bill) Mitchell edited the magazine "Cumbria" from 1951 until 1988. He has contributed articles to the magazine for almost 50 years and has written many books with a Cumbrian setting. "Men of Lakeland", his first hardback, published over 20 years ago, deals with traditional life in the Lakeland dales. J D Marshall, historian, describes it as "one of the most vivid accounts of Cumbrian rural life yet written". Bill received the MBE in the Queen's Honours for services to journalism and to the community in Cumbria and Yorkshire. The University of Bradford awarded him an honorary degree of Doctor of Letters.

SACRED PLACES OF THE LAKE DISTRICT

A Handbook for Holiday Pilgrims

by W R Mitchell

Kind regards
W. R. Mitchell

With a Foreword by Melvyn Bragg

Cartmel.

CASTLEBERG
1999

To the memory of
JIM TAYLOR PAGE
who devoted the sunset of his life
to a study of Cumbrian earth mysteries.

Wᵐ de Wybergh married Elianor yᵉ only Daughter & Sole Heir of Gilbert de Engayne of Clifton in yᵉ County of Weftmorˡᵈ in yᵉ 38. of K.Edwᵈ yᵉ 3ᵈ By wᶜʰ Elianor came yᵉ Manor of Clifton to yᵉ Wyberghs'. 1738.

At Clifton

A **Castleberg** Book.

First published in the United Kingdom in 1999.

Text, © W R Mitchell 1999.

The moral right of the author has been asserted.

ISBN 1 871064 72 4

Typeset in Souvenir, printed and bound in the United Kingdom by Lamberts Print & Design, Station Road, Settle, North Yorkshire, BD24 9AA.

Published by Castleberg, 18 Yealand Avenue, Giggleswick, Settle, North Yorkshire, BD24 0AY.

Contents

When the sweet showers of April fall and shoot
Down through the drought of March to pierce the root,
Bathing every vein in liquid power...
...Then people long to go on pilgrimages
And palmers long to seek the stranger strands
Of far-off saints, hallowed in sundry lands.

Geoffrey Chaucer, The Canterbury Tales,
  from a modern translation.

The Christian Church, with its Mediterranean background,
was like a warm wind blowing from the south; thawing the
frosty north...

Molly Lefebure, Cumbrian Discovery, 1977.

Foreword

by

Melvyn Bragg

Bill Mitchell is one of the alumni of the university of the Lake District. In fact, his half century stint on *Cumbria* makes him one of the longest chroniclers of a place written about so well and over such a span. In short we are in the hands of someone who knows the lie of this land.

The word Sacred is, I am sure, not lightly used, but this book dwells only in part on those places in the district which are 'esteemed especially dear or acceptable to a deity' which my Shorter Oxford Dictionary gives as its first definition of sacred. There are some such places, undoubtedly, and we also have several saints as well as lesser toilers in the several religious denominations which have marked their paths across this mountainous crown of England. We have St Ninian and St Kentigern – both referred to in this book – and there is even a mention of St Bega in whom I can be excused, I hope, a personal interest.

But, rightly, I think, Bill Mitchell takes the landscape, both the landscape of Wordsworth and that of the High Fells as another sacred place. Here too he has the approval of Dictionary authority which says that sacred can also be applied to places and things 'entitled to respect or reverence similar to that which attaches to holy things'. There are any amount of those in the Lake District.

The main point here is that for many visitors the whole district and all that it stands for since the inspiration of Wordsworth is in itself a sacred place – a place where Nature can be experienced in a quite remarkable way, a place in which great beauty and great ease uniquely co-exist, a place to be wondered at.

Whether it is the Castlerigg Stone Circle which comes at the beginning of this book or the Cross Fell which comes near the end, this is a land which can turn visitors into pilgrims and pilgrims who want to – who sometimes feel they have to – return again and again.

For them this book will be a good companion.

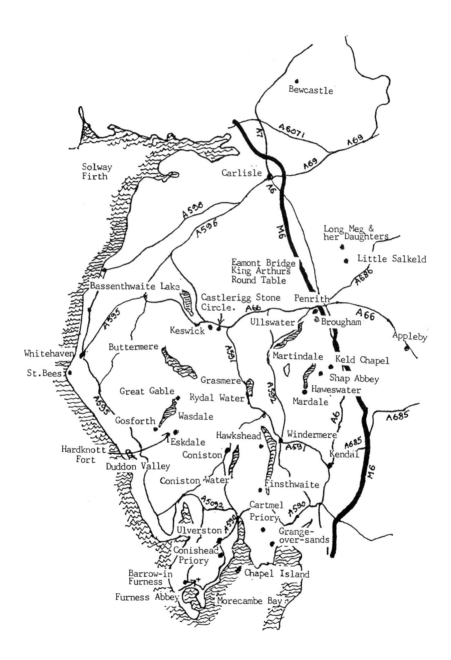

About this Book

The silence that is in the starry sky,
The sleep that is among the lonely hills.

Wordsworth, in his ballad of Brougham Castle.

YOU need not wait, as did Chaucer's pilgrims, until springtime. Travellers on foot or horseback, they craved for warmth, for firm tracks, for bird song and a bounty of flowering plants.

There is something special about the Lakeland spring, when daffodils bloom in the dales but snow still lies in the joints of the great hills. The high dales are like echo chambers for the gruff voices of the ravens. Along the fringes of the fells, a curlew provides the vocal accompaniment. Hanging in the air like a feathered kite, the bird goes into a shallow glide, bubbling over with song.

You may, like Mr Wordsworth, wander "lonely as a cloud", though if a solitary state is preferred a visit to a "honeypot" like Castleberg, the stone circle near Keswick, should occur on a drizzly afternoon in November. At other times of the year, there is no peace for the pilgrim - or for the ghosts of an ancient people.

Winter powders the hills with snow and puts ice into the ancient joints of the mountains. Visitors who arrive to enjoy an alpine atmosphere at Ambleside during Christmas throng the streets. As in Bethlehem, at this time there may be no room at the inn. A warm glow pervades Cartmel Priory when schoolchildren gather round an illuminated tree to sing carols.

In summer, the sun is like a giant searchlight, probing the darkest corners of little Lakeland churches that are normally as quiet as tombs. A beam of light rests on fragments of Anglian crosses adorned by strange creatures from the remote past. The stones have been brought indoors for safety. Morland, south-east of Penrith, has the only Anglo-Saxon church tower left in the county. A contrast in size and magnificence is provided by the Church of the Holy and Undivided Trinity at Carlisle which, like Petra, is built of rose-red sandstone and looks half as old as time.

A pilgrim to the sacred places of Lakeland has the high mobility of a car and the temptation to flit from one place to another. He/she should leave time for contemplation and some physical effort is desirable. The hardy and adventurous doff shoes and stockings to follow Cedric Robinson, guide to Kent Sands, across a low-tide Morecambe Bay.

William Wordsworth wrote that the oversands trip was not just a matter of der-ring-do but a distinct proof of taste. A spell in the wilderness of this "wet Sahara" prepares the mind for the joys of the Promised Land, as indicated by the dove-grey fells of the Lake District which huddle together, as though for mutual comfort, on the northern skyline.

An optional extra, during a pilgrimage to Furness Abbey, is to voyage on a sil-ver-flecked sea in the small boat that operates a ferry service on demand from the tip of Roa Island to Piel. Here, early in the 14th century, the monks built a castle to defend the harbour from the Scots and other raiders. Today's pilgrim can refresh him/herself with a pint at the island pub.

In autumn, the Lake District puts on its coat of many colours. Mist sneaks up the dales. It drifts across features with splendid names, such as Swirral Edge and Catsycam, the last-named being a haunt of wild cats in ancient time. A special occasional effect for the fortunate pilgrim is the Brocken Spectre. In a blaze of low sunlight, a shadowy figure (you) is projected on mist amid rainbow hues.

The pilgrim's feet (or car) might lead him (or her) to Seathwaite, at the head of Borrowdale, from which a sortie can be made by Sour Milk Gill to the summit of Great Gable. The great fell became a sacred place after the 1914-18 war with the appearance of a memorial to members of the Fell and Rock Climbing Club who died while serving in the Forces. At 11 o' clock, on the 11th day of the 11th month, the heads of visitors are bared and bowed for two minutes, sharing in the natural act of remembrance.

The Lake District is relatively small. You might walk across it in a day. In his prime, Joss Naylor, of Wasdale, would cover it on foot in a quarter of the time. When I asked him about his experience of running all the 214 peaks listed as "Wainwrights" in a week, he told me he had "polished off a book a day".

When I first visited Lakeland, this district was divided into three "tribal areas", namely Cumberland, Westmorland and Lancashire North of the Sands. Each had a wedge-shaped piece of the Lakeland "cake". In 1974, when local government was reorganised, the whole area became the county of Cumbria. With water on three sides and the River Eden on the fourth side, Cumbria is almost an island, for Solway Firth, the Irish Sea and Morecambe Bay wash its shores.

Mysterious Lakeland

The history of Cumbria cannot be properly understood as a series of airtight compartments known as "centuries". New ideas flow. Old beliefs linger with no regard for our rigid concept of time. Everyone loves a mystery. In these Lakeland jaunts, the pilgrim will encounter mysteries galore, with much scope for theorising.

There is interest in trying to sort out a tangled web of fact and supposition. The imagination is stretched by the experience of standing in a stone circle some 4,000 years old or by a stone cross on which the battle of ideas between Christianity and the ancient beliefs are presented as carved figures.

Who carved the figures on the slender redstone cross in Gosforth churchyard? Was there really a saint called Bega after whom St Bees headland was named? How did St Martin become associated with t'auld chapel in Martindale? Was Patterdale named after St Patrick or could it have been a crusty old Norseman?

The men who wrote down accounts of the Christian saints – in some cases, a century or two after the events described – were monks. In the days when the saints bestrode the North, they were among the few literate people. Naturally, they Christianised the pagan narratives and, when dealing with their subjects, would add a few stories to further exalt the memory of the saints.

Clouded with Superstition

Lakeland folk, like most northerners, were a superstitious lot. The first person to cross the threshhold on New Year's Day must be a dark-haired man who, in a custom known as first-footing, was regaled with food and wine. The rural imagination conjured up ghosts, fairies and even an army of troops, marching five abreast, on the eastern side of the summit of Souter Fell. This is said to have occurred on Midsummer Eve, 1735. What matter if the terrain was unsuitable for military manoevres? Why spoil a good story by inquiring further into the facts?

Anyone who heard three distinct raps were on the wall of a house shivered, for it presaged a death in the family. You must take care how you handled glass vessels kept at certain houses. They were known as "lucks" – ill-lucks, if dropped. You will find an illustration of the Luck of Edenhall on a wall of the local church, which has a parkland setting half a mile from the village. The glass is now in the Victoria and Albert Museum in London, but tales about it are still told locally. Should the glass have been broken, then ill luck would have come upon its owners, the wealthy Musgrave family.

How did the glass come into their possession? It may have been a souvenir of the Crusades, though local people were convinced it was found in the possession of fairies by the Musgrave butler who had been sent to draw water at a well known to be a haunt of the wee folk. The butler grabbed the cup. The fairies sang: "Whene'er this cup shall break or fall, farewell the luck of Edenhall." In the end, it was the family mansion, not the Luck, that perished. It burnt down.

On the way to this little church, which is dedicated to St Cuthbert, you pass the Plague Cross, marking the site of a stone basin. In the latter part of the 16th century, this is said to have been filled with vinegar. Sufferers from the plague (typhus?) put their money into it to cleanse it when collecting food brought to them by the good folk of Penrith. Before the plague had run its course, it had claimed a quarter of the villagers.

The Need-fire

Among the strange beliefs that lingered through the centuries, long before the age of veterinary science, was the "need-fire", kindled to purify cattle suffering from a disease such as murrain. William Pearson, of Crosthwaite, near Kendal, a friend of the Wordsworths, met a Winster farmer who had been present when a living calf was sacrificed by fire. This apparently had been the custom in Celtic times.

The need-fire was reported at a late date from Crosthwaite and Cartmel Fell. Doreen Wallace, in *English Lakeland* (1940), mentioning the use of the need-fire in the Keswick district as lately as 1841, described it as "one of a number of surviving half-magic methods." When it was required, every fire in the village was put out, inspectors going round to all the houses to see that not a spark remained. In an open space, two pieces of wood were set alight by friction, a fire was kindled and the cattle either driven through it or assembled on the smoky side so they would get plenty of the "reek". Harriet Martineau, one of the notable Victorian writers in Lakeland, told of a farmer who, when all his cattle had their dose of the need-fire, drove his ailing wife through it.

Celtic Customs

Who were the first pilgrims? They were possibly stimulated by tales told of the Crusades. Now that television – a modern equivalent of the Tower of Babel – fills the air with raucous sounds, the notion of having a quiet excursion to a holy place, where one might be reflective and in tune with the natural world is attractive. Many have developed an interest in the Celtic way of life because it was Nature, not a drive to make more and more cash, that dictated their mood and pace.

They worshipped at rivers and springs. Cumbria abounds with springs. My old friend Jim Taylor Page, to whom I dedicate this book, surveyed many underground springs in relation to stone circles and early church sites. Jim found over 1,500 springs – many of them "holy" – marked as "Spr" on the Ordnance Survey 1:25,000 maps of the county.

Sacred Places of the Lake District contains details of 26 mini-pilgrimages, in or immediately around the picturesque core of Cumbria. Many of them are at the edge of the Cumbrian dome, now widely known as the English Lake District. In some cases there will be a fell-country background. Apart from the obvious benefit of healthy exercise, away from the main tourist attractions, there is a tingle-factor in contemplating the events and mysteries of past ages, prompted by stone circles, holy wells, stone crosses, hogshead tombstones, figures in stained glass and sacred mountains.

Some ancient tracks have been macadamised and are roads along which traffic passes with a whine and a whoosh. Others are still covered by verdant green, though even here traffic, in the shape of small all-terrain vehicles, is wiping its feet. A favourite old track was originally known as the Bretestrete – the way of the Britons – connecting Troutbeck near Windermere with the Penrith area. The Romans used it as a route between Brougham and Troutbeck.

The last recommended pilgrimage in this book is to an unpretentious window-ledge memorial to St Alfred (Wainwright), who denounced religion but in his writings about the mountains of Lakeland and Scotland revealed some spiritual qualities. From Buttermere Church, where he is commemorated, we will climb on to Hay Stacks and stand by the tarn near where his ashes were scattered. A rambler friend has a theory that, Hay Stacks being very popular, it would not be long before those ashes had been transferred, on the boots of walkers, to the floor of the pub bar in the village.

Finding Your Way

Invest in the four Outdoor Leisure maps covering The English Lakes and published by the Ordnance Survey. At $2^1/2$" to the mile (4cm to 1km) they are specially designed for a popular recreation area. Acquaint yourself with the route in advance of a visit so that blundering is minimised.

In some cases, grid references (presented as GR before a number) will be provided. Details of how to assess the numbers are found printed on OS maps, but an easily remembered rule is "evening comes before night". Use East, then North, when working out the grid references. The footpaths are clearly shown as hatched green lines. A good pilgrim must not trespass, though a little blundering is permitted.

Learn how to use a compass in relation to your Ordnance Survey map. Pack in a rucksack some durable clothes – perhaps even a bivvy bag. The weather on the fells is, to say the least, variable, and might change from sunshine to stinging hail in minutes.

"Curious" Visitors

The Lakers are those persons who visit the
beautiful scenes in Cumberland and Westmorland
by distinction styled the Lakes.

From a comic opera, 1798.

A PILGRIM is defined as "one who journeys to a sacred place as an act of religious devotion". In this book, the pilgrim is deemed to be a visitor to
Lakeland who breaks away from touristy pursuits and seeks out those places
where the spirit is uplifted by thoughts of "saints who from their labours rest."

De Quincey was one of the Lake Poets who found inspiration in nature. The
sight of a huge boulder by Kirkstone Pass prompted one of his splendid fantasies.
He wrote: "This mimic church...has a peculiarly fine effect in this wild situation,
which leaves so far below the tumults of this world." It suggested "the phantom
and evanescent image of a congregation, where never congregation met; of the
pealing organ, where never sound was heard except of wild natural notes, or else
of the wind rushing through these mighty gates of everlasting rock..."

From nature triumphant, we move on to stone circles, which represent man's
first permanent mark on the landscape. Thousands of years have passed since the
big stones were reared up and many of them remain, like ancient molars on gums
of green. Christianity arrived with the Romans and William Camden, compiler of
Britannia, the first detailed description of Britain (1586), found the Roman period
enthralling, even though when visiting the site of Galava, at the head of
Windermere, he found that with the departure of the Romans it had become "the
carcase as it were of an antient city".

Camden thrilled at the sight of "great ruins of walls, and of buildings without
the walls still remaining scattered about...the mortar mixed with fragments of
brick, the small urns, glass vessels, Roman coins and the paved roads."

The first of the "curious travellers" in the Lake District was a young woman
called Celia Fiennes, who at the end of the 17th century was commenting on

people, buildings, the state of the roads and, of course, the grand scenery. She was able to form her own opinions for as yet there was little or no observations by travellers – those who had the taste and leisure to explore secluded corners of their native land. In the Penrith area, Celia made a special point of visiting the stone circle known as Long Meg and her Daughters.

Daniel Defoe (c1720) made some earthy comments and was not thrilled by the mountains. Westmorland was to him "a county eminent only for being the wildest, most barren and frightful of any...in England." He was more attracted to the fertile parties of Cumberland and to the brisk trade in fresh-run salmon in the Derwent and Eden. Relays of fast horses conveyed a goodly proportion to London.

Beauty, horror, immensity united were three circumstances that Dr John Brown mentioned when describing "the full perfection" of Keswick in a letter to Lord Lyttelton (1753). Brown, who made an annual visit to the Lake District as "a religious act", added: "But to give you a complete idea of these three perfections as they are joined in Keswick would require the united powers of Claude, Salvator and Poussin..."

An article in the *Gentleman's Magazine* of 1748 extolled the virtues of the Windermere area. The quest was both for antiquities and glimpses of Wild Lakeland, with its rugged crags and raging torrents. As yet, the only fell-walkers were shepherds tending their little herdwick sheep.

First Guide Book

The first pilgrim in a religious sense was possibly Thomas West (c1720-79), a Scot who trained as a Jesuit priest at the English College in Liege. It was West who produced the first guide book to the area (1778) and developed the idea of "stations". These were the recommended vantage points, the term "station" doubtless being prompted by the concept of The Stations of the Cross.

West lived at Lindal in Furness and, being chaplain at Titcup Hall, near Dalton, was handy for visits to the impressive ruins of Furness Abbey, which had been one of the greatest in the land and a "must" for the early tourist. (As yet, Barrow had not evolved from a tiny village into an industrial town).

The observations of Thomas Gray (1716-1771) during tour in the Lake District in search of the picturesque (1769) were printed as *Journal of the Lakes*, stimulating others with a taste for wild places to follow (almost literally) in his footsteps. William Hutchinson (1772) included Long Meg in his itinerary and found Keswick was "a mean village" with "very indifferent accommodation for travellers."

Early seekers for the Picturesque carried the Claude-glass, a convex mirror, some four inches in diameter. Standing with his back to the scenery, a pilgrim could see the landscape reduced to the size of a postcard, the shape and perspective being thus revealed at a glance. William Westall, an artist of renown, produced *Views of the Lake and Vale of Keswick*, which helped to stimulate a print-selling industry.

The Lakers

Towards the end of the century, the Rev James Plumptre, a Fellow of Clare College, Cambridge, undertook three walking tours and penned a satirical play entitled *The Lakers*. When Wordsworth wrote his guide (1822) he "consulted nature and my feelings". In turn, Grasmere became a major focal point for tourism for visitors seeking places associated with William Wordsworth.

Local people would wonder what all the fuss was about. One of them observed: "I see they've letten out Wordsworth again." The Poet must have presented a strange sight in his later days as, shuffling along, wearing a straw hat, shading his weak eyes, he muttered while composing his poems. A description of Wordsworth, as seen by young John Ruskin at Crosthwaite Church, includes this passage:

> *His hair was no colour at all by the way,*
> *But half of't was black, slightly scattered with grey;*
> *His eyes were as black as coal, but in turning*
> *They flashed – aye, as much as that coal does in burning...*

Wordsworth lived "as regularly as clockwork; indeed, more regularly than our own clocks, which go all paces."

A Tidier Landscape

By the 1830s, the tourist trade was under way, with new roads and great mobility provided by faster and safer coach and posting services. At a few hotels,

Porch of Aspatria Church (1814).

horses and carriages were available so that visitors might explore the district without getting exhausted. The Lakeland they saw had a much tidier appearance than was experienced by the early tourists. The difference was provided by drystone walls – hundreds of miles of walls made without a dab of mortar, a consequence of the enclosure of the commons with Parliamentary approval.

Mr Crosthwaite's Museum at Keswick gave such visitors an awareness of history and tradition. Visitors also noticed the marks of industry, including adits and slag heaps, for the district had been ransacked for copper, lead, iron ore and slate. These had been ignored by Wordsworth in his celebrated guide. He had made general comments about industrialisation. He did not care much for "the inventions and universal applications of machinery". He denounced the fashion for plantations as "vegetable manufactury".

From the 1840s, there was a steamer service across Morecambe Bay to Barrow and Ulverston. Rail links were established, the line to Windermere being opened in April, 1847, and the Furness Railway Company binding the northern shore of the Bay in bands of steel a few years later. The Windermere line had a profound effect on central Lakeland.

Wordsworth feared that the transportation of large numbers of people into the heart of the Lake District would destroy the amenity they came to enjoy. The railway company replied that whereas there would be a crowd around the terminus, the rest of the district would be unaffected by tourist pressures. The railhead was at Birthwaite, which soon blossomed under the name Windermere.

Victorian development, if not the railway, spread northwards, leading to a rash of building. Ambleside is almost exclusively a Victorian town, its principal church appearing to stand on tip-toe as it extends its lofty spire towards heaven.

Sporting Types

Lakeland, which once over-awed the visitor, became a setting for sport and recreation. Climbing, originally popular with university types, who had adequate spare time, was given publicity by Owen Glynne Jones in his *Rock Climbing in the English Lake District*, published in 1897. The photographs illustrating it were the work of two Keswick men, Ashley and George Abraham.

The outdoor movement took off in the 1930s when Lakeland was re-discovered by a host of people living in the industrial towns. The Youth Hostels'

Association provided inexpensive accommodation. In recent times, Mr Wainwright produced his inimitable guides to the Lakeland fells and soon old tracks were being eroded by booted battalions. Wainwright claimed he was just meeting a demand which would have happened anyway.

Now it is the glossy brochure and the colourful film on television that prompt people to join the Lakeland throng in summer. If Wordsworth lived at a time when nature and the enterprises of man were in attractive balance, now man appears to have the upper hand. Yet today's pilgrim may still find the quiet places where the old feelings of awe and reverence are stirred.

Mysterious Beginnings

The stone circles mark a significant change in Man's awareness of himself, for now for the first time he was building something which would outlast his own lifespan.

William Rollinson (1984)

TODAY, when sodium chloride lighting gives the urban areas of the Lake District an overall orange hue, and stains the underbellies of the clouds, it is not easy to imagine the experience of the first human settlers at the approach of darkness. In winter, the air would shiver with the contact-calls of wolves. The flickering Northern Lights and the cold, unblinking stare of the moon in a sky patterned by stars would offer little light.

Emotionally, the people would be fully developed, to judge by cave paintings on the Continent and the stone circles to be found at Castlerigg, near Keswick, and around the edges of the Lake District. The idea of megaliths in a mountain setting is a great concept. Yet only Castlerigg fits this description, situated on a tract of level ground, ringed by some of the shapeliest fells in the Lake District. Megalith, from the Greek, means "great stones". The largest stone circle, Long Meg and her Daughters, has a glorious situation near Little Salkeld, between Lakeland and the Northern Pennines.

The People

The fore-elders of those who arranged the stones in Lakeland had migrated in stages from the shores of the eastern Mediterranean. In Brittany, they constructed stone avenues, circles and tombs. One group of migrants, following the west coast of England, left a scattering of stone circles. They were hunters who dabbled in farming during a period when the climate was appreciably dry and warm.

Making a round hut with a low stone wall and cone-shaped thatched roof was within the capability of a family. The landscape was littered with stony debris from the glaciers. A stone circle demanded corporate effort. How were the megaliths

21

shifted into position?

The Neolithic (New Stone Age) settlers who built so durably were hunters who dabbled in farming. They opened up the landscape using the slash-and-burn technique. They slaughtered birds and animals for food and doubtless fished in the lakes. There would be wild rejoicing if a red deer was brought down, for it represented some 300 lb of good red meat. The skin and antlers could be converted into useful domestic objects.

Places of Assembly

In Neolithic times, when the stone circles appeared, the human population living in favoured places at the periphery of the Lakeland mountains would not number more than 2,000. Early people were not unduly aware of straight lines; they saw the curves of high hills hunching themselves against westerly gales; they witnessed the orbs of sun and moon. In an atmosphere clear of pollutants, stars twinkled against the black arc of the sky.

We will never know the true purpose of the stone circles. My old friend Jim Taylor-Page, in his *A Field Guide to the Lake District* (1984), favoured the "place of assembly" theory, adding: "Undoubtedly pagan ceremonials took place and religious fervour must have been a primary incentive." Whatever form worship took, it was an expression of a human need to pay homage to a superior being.

Victorian writers, who thought of the circles as a setting for tribal gatherings, stressed the religious aspect. At the end of winter, as the world was about to be plunged into perpetual darkness, there must have been general relief when Something or Someone gave the sun a nudge, put leaves on the trees and made the birds sing.

Many believe the stone circles were simply astronomical observation points by which the yearly round of activity might be planned. Charlie Emet, who has written extensively about the Eden Valley, has noticed that often in the larger megalithic rings there are larger stones at the main compass points. At Long Meg, only due east and west are marked in this way. "To the Neolithic arable farmers and stockbreeders looking for signs of the return of warmer weather, this was very important, for at the spring and autumn equinoxes, half-way between its summer and winter solstices, the sun rises in the east and sets in the west."

If they were calendars and temples combined, what sort of deity had early people in mind when they raised great stones at Castlerigg or created Long Meg and her inscrutable brood? Why should an ancient people have expended so much time and energy on operations unconnected with basic living – with shelter and finding sufficient food?

Today, when Castlerigg is thronged by chattering tourists, it is difficult to imagine an ancient world in which there were no maps, no books, and when man was among the frailest creatures on the scene. I imagine the builders of the stone circles to have been little, dark folk. Just how they assembled and raised such large stones is now a matter of speculation. With no means of recording their experiences, as through writing, tales of the circles would be passed on by word of mouth, becoming increasingly garbled until, a century or more later, they had gathered the moss of imaginative story-telling.

Mysteries Remain

If the stone circles were at tribal centures, their situation gives us an idea of the density and distribution of the population in Neolithic times. Frank Haley, observing that some of the Lakeland standing stones are "uphill", wrote: "In prehistoric times, high living was obligatory. The pearly smoothness of Derwentwater and the jet suavity of Wastwater today each provides a brilliant metamorphosis of the jungle-choked, swampy, insect and animal-ridden pools they were before historic man cleared the valleys and bared the fellsides. Primitive man lived perforce on higher, healthier and safer ground."

Waterhouse records 66 stone circles or circle sites in Cumbria. The majority are located in the more fertile lower lands where settlements abounded as agriculture and pastoralism developed in the Neolithic era. Sixteen of the total are now lost in their original form. Little has been found in or about the stone circles. Treasure-seekers or antiquarians will have destroyed some of the evidence. Burnmoor's glorious complex of standing stones was, like many another, re-cycled, the stones appearing in more modern structures.

A circle which is the equal of Castlerigg in size but is tucked well away from a motor road, below Black Combe, is known as Swinside, also Sunkenkirk (GR 172883). Over 50 stones embedded in a firm layer of pebbles form a tight circle on open land. Approach Swinside on foot along a minor road extending from the west side of the road between Duddon Bridge and Millom. The circle is viewable from a footpath but the land on which it stands is private. Swinside was a favourite place of William Wordsworth, to whom it was

that mystic Round of Druid frame
tardily sinking by its proper weight
deep into patient Earth, from whose smooth breast it came!

At Shap, a stone circle known as Shap Stones or Karl Lofts, was damaged when the London and North Western Railway was driven through the area in the 19th century. Here were two great circles, connected by long avenues of single stones. Two other standing stones in the Shap area are the Boggleby Stone (beside a path between Shap and Keld) and the Thunder Stone, just off the road to Rosgill.

Near some of the stone circles are what remain of the long-cairns built in the early Neolithic period – a wedge-shaped mound with a burial chamber at the eastern end. The stone circles and the long-cairns must have seemed immeasurely old to the folk who lived a millenium later, by which time tribes under powerful chiefs felt a need for security and created the hill fort.

Pilgrimage 1 – Castlerigg Stone Circle

GR 291236. A National Trust property, cared for by English Heritage, 1½ miles east of Keswick. Access from the old A66 (Keswick-Penrith) road.

Basic Details

Castlerigg means "the fort on the ridge". The circle, formerly known as The Carles, is located at about 700 ft above sea level, the ridge lying between the Greta and the foot of Blencathra The big stones, of volcanic rock, were shifted to this area by glacial ice. Some were positioned in a circle by the folk of late Neolithic or early Bronze Age, some 4,000 years ago, and were possibly used for astronomical purposes.

Castlerigg is not a true circle, the diameter varying from 100 to 110 ft.

Originally there were about 50 stones. Now there are 38, with 10 stones forming a rectangle at the south side. There is a slight hollow at the centre.

Folk Lore

In the romantic age, from about 1760, Castlerigg was linked with the Druids. Keats described Castlerigg in 1818 as -

> *...a dismal cirque*
> *Of Druid stones upon a forlorn moor,*
> *When the chill rain begins at shut of eve*
> *In dull weather.*

Early Pilgrims

Thomas Gray (1769) saw the stones rising from a crop of corn. Arrayed before him was "a Druid circle of large stones, one hundred and eight feet in diameter, the biggest not eight feet high, but most of them still erect: they are fifty in number." As the sun broke out of cloud, Gray discovered "the most enchanting view I have yet seen of the whole valley behind me, the two lakes, the river, the mountains in all their glory."

Keats and Brown (1818) incorporated a visit as part of a much longer walk. They had "a fag up hill, rather too near dinner time, which was rendered void, by the gratification of seeing those aged stones, on a gentle rise in the midst of Mountains..." Robert Southey (1829), writing of "the Druidical Stones", mentioned that "the circle is of the rudest kind, consisting of single stones, unhewn, and chosen without any regard to shape of magnitude, being of all sizes."

Pilgrim's Way

Call at the Information Office at the Moot Hall, in central Keswick, then (as shown on English Lakes map, North West) head out of town south-eastwards towards Castleberg Farm. After walking beside a row of stylish houses you will ascend by path through Springs Wood, passing close to a metal mast. With Castlerigg Farm on your left, follow the path through to the A591 and cross over to enter Castle Lane.

Castlerigg Stone Circle is clearly seen where the end of a remarkably straight stretch of road forms a T junction with another road near Goosewell Farm. Return to Keswick from the stone circle on a field path running parallel and to the east of Castle Lane, heading for High Nest and then the A591. Turn right. A little roadwork is necessary before the footpath used on the outward journey is encountered (left) and you begin a scenic descent to Keswick.

Pilgrimage 2 – Long Meg and her Daughters

GR 571372. Approached from the A685 (Penrith-Alston) road, which should be left at Langwathby for Little Salkeld. Now follow the Glassonby road and turn left at a cul de sac which is signposted. The road leads through part of the stone circle to Long Meg Farm.

Basic Details

The circumference of the main circle is 365m and there are rather more than 70 granite stones. Count them twice, get the same number – and they will return to life! The average weight is 10 tons and the heaviest has been assessed at 28 tons. Meg, a block of red sandstone 12ft/4m high, stands distinct from the main group, which is composed of granite.

Faint markings on Meg's ruddy face include a cup and ring with gutter and concentric circles. They may have been added in later times. Little Meg, a much smaller circle, half a mile away, on private land, incorporated a burial site. Jim Taylor Page, who studied stone circles intensely, thought Long Meg and her brood might have been used for both astronomical purposes and funerary rites.

Romantic Tales

Tradition says the circle was a coven of witches turned to stone by a vengeful angel. Another fanciful tale claims the granite stones of the circle were lovers of Meg. "She" is said to bleed if a piece is broken from her but, of course, you would break the pilgrim's unwritten code if you damaged her. A small boy who was shown concentric circles on Meg asked: "Does that mean they were made in Japan?"

Early Pilgrims

Drayton, in Poly-Olbion recorded that -

Stones seventie seven stand, in manner of a Ring,
Each full ten foot in height, but yet the strangest thing,
Their equall distance is, the circle that compose,
Within which other stones lye flat, which doe inclose
The bones of men long dead (as there the people say).

Wordsworth (1821) chanced upon the stones and afterwards wrote:

A weight of awe, not easily to be borne,
Fell suddenly upon my Spirit – cast
From the dread bosom of the unknown past,
When first I saw that family forlorn...

He addressed the stone named Meg: "Speak, Giant Mother". She maintained her enigmatic silence.

Pilgrim's Way

Spread the walk over several miles of varied scenery by parking the car at Little Salkeld and heading northwards on a track adjacent to the Settle-Carlisle railway to where evidence is found of Long Meg Mine. A man who once farmed the land beside the Stone Circle when the anhydrite mine was active could, in the stillness of night, hear the sounds of men working the late shift in the mine.

The path reaches the bank of the Eden and continues to the road connecting Lazonby with Glassonby. Turn right for Glassonby and from the churchyard, which is a little way from the village, follow a footpath which leads across open country to Long Meg.

Pilgrimage 3 – King Arthur's Round Table

GR 519284. At Eamont Bridge, just south of Penrith. This feature and the even more stupendous Mayburgh are situated on either side of B5230, the

road leading from Eamont Bridge to Newby Bridge and Ullswater. Both
archaeological features are in the care of English Heritage.

Basic Details

The Round Table is a Bronze Age henge site and therefore considerably older
than the period during which King Arthur is said to have existed. The site was
dated by reference to a bronze and a stone axe found at the site. It is possible that
the Arthurian connection was introduced by the Clifford family, who had much
land and property at Brougham. The first of the Cliffords took his name from a
village on the Welsh Marches and a descent from King Arthur would be claimed.

Celia Fiennes in 1698 saw "a banke round it like a bench...Its story is that it
was the table a great Giant 6 yards tall used to feed at and there entertained
another of nine yards tall which he afterwards killed." Leland (1540) had supposed
it to be the remains of a "castel". Local people used the Round Table for various
competitive games until last century. All traces of a former Little Round Table
have been lost.

Nearby Mayburgh, a henge site, is believed to have been created between
2,000 and 1,000 BC. The 15 ft bank, formed of rounded stones taken from the
river, surrounds an area of about $1^1/_2$ acres. A nine-feet high stone is the sole sur-
vivor of "four stones of great magnitude" noted by John Aubrey and described by
William Stukeley as being "of a hard black kind of stone, like the altar at
Stonehenge." It is said that about the year 1775 a local man blew up three of the
stones "by gunpowder" to amuse himself.

Romantic Associations

Mayburgh had the usual association with Druids. Sir Walter Scott, in The Bridal
of Triermain, wrote:

> *For feats of chivalry renown'd,*
> *Left Mayborough's mound and stones of power,*
> *By Druids raised in magic hour,*
> *And traced the Eamont's winding way,*
> *Till Ulfo's lake beneath him lay.*

Coleridge described Mayburgh as "a scene of religion and seclusion." This hardly applies today, close to Eamont Bridge, where traffic over the old bridge is controlled by coloured lights.

Pilgrim's Way

Consult the OS map for The English Lakes (North Eastern Area). Leave the car at Sockbridge, beside the B5320, just south of Penrith. A path strikes northwards through fields to a bank of the River Eamont. Follow a path eastwards, passing between historic Yanwath Hall and the hamlet of that name.

The remainder of the walk is through park-like countryside, returning to the riverside and using a bridge under the M6. Beyond the bridge, bear right, passing between gateposts surmounted by stone eagles to where a sign indicates Mayburgh. The Round Table lies across the road beyond. Both have been clearly marked by English Heritage and each has an instructional sign.

Christians Awake!

CHRISTIANITY arrived in north-west England with the Romans about the year 80 AD. Their empire stretched from the Great Wall to North Africa and, with Agricola as their military commander, they entered a region they would occupy for nearly three and a-half centuries.

What is now Cumbria was tenanted by the Cymry or Celtic folk, farmers and herdsmen who lived mainly at the fringes of the mountain block and were especially numerous in the northern area, to which they would give a name – Cumberland. The Celts were a stoical, close-knit race, with a sense of national identity. Tacitus, a Roman historian, wrote of them as having "swarthy faces, with a tendency for their hair to curl." Jim Taylor Page, who was fascinated by the Celtic period of Cumbrian history, described the Celts as "stocky, with round head, dark eyes, broad face and dark hair", features which, he thought, might be detected in some of the people living today.

The Romans by and large left the Celts to themselves and their nature gods. They interfered only if they felt threatened. So many of the Celts remained heathen, an unlovely term. They did at least respect their environment, worshipping the gods of nature - of woods, rivers and springs.

A good Roman, having given to the Emperor the things that belonged to the Emperor was then able to select a god for special attention. For example, the officer class of the Roman Army had a fondness for the cult of Mithras which, like Christianity, had sprung from the east. A stone temple to Mithras stood near Hadrian's Wall. Three altars were in place and on the central altar was a colourful representation of the Sun God.

We know a little about the symbolism but nothing of the inner mysteries. A sense of mystery was sustained in a darkened temple when a lamp was placed behind that central altar, with its representation of Mithras, so that rays shone from the Sun God's crown. The air in the temple was made fragrant by burning fir cones brought specially from North Africa.

Nature Worship

The settlements of the Celtic folk consisted of circular huts with stone bases and spired roofs of wood and thatch. Celtic fields were small and rectangular. Cattle, sheep and pigs were kept. The Celts worshipped the black horse or pony. The Celts were a sophisicated people, referred to by a modern writer, Molly Lefebure, as "a people of vast creative energy, of poetry and imagination."

Part of the Celtic bequest were the names of some of our rivers – Derwent, Crake, Esk and Eden. Four annual festivals, including May Day (Beltane) marked the Celtic year, when sacrifices were offered to Baal, whom they knew by the name of Grannus. Placate the god and there would be fertility among the herds and good harvests from the fields.

Roman Ways

In the Lake District, the Romans maintained their presence largely through roads and attendant cohort forts, from which they policed the area. Each fort housed about 500 men. A major trans-Lakeland route extended from Watercrook, in the Lune Valley, to Ambleside, which the Romans called Galava, thence over the passes of Wrynose and Hardknott to the valley of the Esk and Ravenglass, a port by the western sea.

The Romans were fond of creature comforts. Though traces of the fort at Ravenglass were to be destroyed by Victorian railway-builders, much of the bath-house endures and is impressive enough for it to have become known as Walls Castle. Roman foot soldiers trudged along a road which had evolved from the Brethstrett, "the paved way of the Britons", crossing – though not quite at the summit – the fell now known as High Street, over 2,000 ft above sea level. This was a useful link between Brougham, in the Eden Valley, and Waterhead, in central Lakeland.

A scattering of indigenous people would stare with lower jaws drooping with amazement as a contingent of Roman troops went by. The finest troops were kept at the legionary centres, such as York, and the roadside forts were garrisoned by auxillaries, who had been recruited in lands beside the Mediterranean. It was not considered prudent to allow men to serve in the country of their birth.

The soldiers who marched towards the Brethstrett from Edenvale would doubtless shiver at the sight of ancient tumuli scattered across a broad saddle at Moor

Major Roman Roads

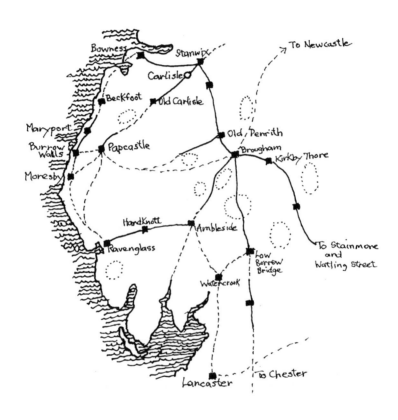

Roman Road

Possible Route

Celtic Settlement

Fort

Walled Town

Divock and especially at Cockpit, a ringlet of 20 large stones, looking half as old as time. What strange rites had taken place there?

The Romans did not subdue Scotland. Nor did they set foot in Ireland. After an unsuccessful sortie into Scotland, they kept a tight military grip on the northern border, the system hingeing on Hadrian's Wall, and attendant defensive systems that extended from sea to sea across the "neck" of Britain. Not only did it seal off Scotland, with its troublesome Picts, but it gave the Empire a specific border in north-west Europe.

The wall and the military zone immediately behind it ensured that good Romans further south might sleep safely in their beds. They also provided ideal conditions for the spread of the new religion. Most of the tombstones of Roman times had invoked "the spirits of the departed". Despite their "mod cons", many Romans died relatively young. Anicus Ingenuus, a doctor of Housesteads, was but 25 years old. Aurelia Aureliana did rather better, achieving an age of 41. Her matronly figure, holding a bunch of poppies, was portrayed on her tombstone.

"WELCOME BACK TO CUMBRIA, FLAVIUS —ENJOY YOUR LEAVE IN SUNNY NAPLES?"

Among the debris of a lost Empire was a stone inscribed to the memory of Flavius Antigonus Papias, who died at Carlisle. A man of Greek origin, he was probably a Christian. Titus, another follower of Christ whose name was inscribed on stone, lived at Brougham, in the Eden Valley. Christianity became the official religion of the Roman Empire after an edict of Emperor Constantine in the early part of the 4th century. The Romans tolerated religious beliefs of any kind provided any of them did not lead to disrespect for the Emperor.

Who first breathed the name of Christ in the dark, dank, misty northern borderland? Could it have been one of the soldiers drafted to the Wall? Or perhaps a Roman official promoted to a position of trust in a major settlement like Carlisle? Was the Word discussed in the forts of Brougham or Ambleside or by a traveller who, having made a chilling journey across the grain of the Lake District, languished in a reflective mood at the bathhouse of Ravenglass. In about the year 200 AD, one Tertullian noted that "parts of the Britains inaccessible to the Romans were indeed conquered by Christ."

When the Wall was abandoned in 383AD; when the Lakeland forts of Galava and Mediobogdum were deserted and Roman troops no longer patrolled the road to the sea, the Celtic way of life re-asserted itself. There were pure-blooded Celts and others in whom the blood of Celt and Roman had been intermixed through the marriage of a native girl to one of the veterans of the Roman Army who had acquired Roman citizenship because of exemplary service.

With the Wall and its attendant structures forsaken, an old tribal system re-asserted itself, though the Britons who sustained it had become largely Romanised. In the so-called Dark Ages, Christianity hung on by a thread.

Wilderness Ways

There were some who, inspired by the "desert fathers" of the Middle East, preserved the simplicity and purity of the faith by emulating Christ and returning to the wilderness. They were the inspiration behind the decision of some pious Celts to live in wild places on the western seaboard, which was also the north-west rim of Europe. These "deserts" were enlivened by the cries of the sea birds and the boom of waves breaking against weed-strewn rocks.

In late Celtic times, Christian communities on specks of land off the coasts of Ireland and Scotland worshipped the Christian God cheerfully, with a disregard for their own bodily state and needs. Their knees were calloused from long prayerful sessions during which their eyes were inclined heavenwards. Their resolution was tested during hazardous sea crossings in craft made of wood and animal hides.

These Celtic saints were at one with God and Nature. The most devout were regarded as saints not through some Papal decree but because (as it was said of St Cuthbert) they were "wholly bent on heavenly things." Through missionary activity, the Word spread back to northern England.

New Settlers

The Celtic twilight was an uneasy period. With the threat of raids from the north, hill forts were inhabited. They were to acquire the prefix Castle, hence Castle Head, Castle Crag, Castle How. Anglian settlers spread to the Eden Valley, to the Cumberland Plain and to Cartmel from Northumbria.

St Ninian crossed from Scotland and exuberantly preached the Christian message, possibly at Brougham, near Penrith, where in Roman times there had been an important crossing point of major roads. In the 10th century, long after the Romans had quit the land, Norse settlers arrived and many Celts abandoned their settlements and moved to Cambria (Wales).

The Norse folk were unopposed when they claimed the very heads of the dales and cleared the land. They established farms and had saeters (summer grazings) on the fells. Norse folk were eventually coaxed from their old gods by the appeal of the Christian church. The Anglian farmers, converted to Christianity, left an account of their spiritual struggles on carved stone crosses, such as those at Bewcastle, Gosforth and Irton.

Pilgrimage 4 – Hardknott Roman Fort

GR 218014. Hardknott stands eyrie-like at the western end of Hardknott Pass, which connects Eskdale with the upper Duddon at Cockley Beck. It is owned by the National Trust but is in the care of English Heritage, who have provided interpretive panels. The poet Auden compared this fort with a motionless eagle eyeing the valley. Wordsworth (1820) wrote of "that lone camp on Hardknott's height, whose guardians bow the knee to Jove and Mars." Perhaps there was someone at Hardknott who bowed the knee to Christ.

Basic Details

Hardknott, which the Romans knew as Mediobogdum [fort in the middle of the curve], guarded the road that cut across the grain of Lakeland between the forts at Waterhead (Ambleside) and Ravenglass. At an elevation of 800 ft., it occupied the only available spur beneath a fell cresting at 1,500ft. On 30 acres of ground, the Roman engineers built a three-acre stone fort, complete with stone granary and headquarters building. The soldiers were housed in wooden barrack blocks.

The fort, with a typical playing-card shape, was completed early in the reign of Hadrian (117-138 AD) by the 4th cohort of Dalmatians, part of the former Yugo Slavia. The gates are of an unusual plan, lacking guard chambers. They were fashioned of red sandstone, wrenched from living rock at the coast.

The fort had the usual Roman luxury of a bath-house, or balneum, though it was small by Roman standards. A succession of graded temperature rooms derived heat from a stokehole.

Hardknott Pass

It connects Eskdale with the Duddon Valley and is not for the faint-hearted. From Eskdale, in one mile, the road attains an elevation of 1,000 ft. A motorist travelling from the Duddon has to cope with a gradient as acute as 1 in 3 and a succession of S-bends. The road authority does not attempt to keep it clear of snow in winter. In summer, there are usually too many cars in limited space.

Observations

Mary Fair, who lived at Holmrook, wrote papers on the fort, offering a possible chronology within the Roman period. This moving passage is from her description of Hardknott:

"As you reach the shattered remnant of the once busy Roman fort, you look across the dark rift of the Upper Eskdale Valley to the piled crests and peaks of the high mountains. Upon them the shafts of the rising sun strike lights and glints of a fairyland never seen at any other time of the day. Many a Roman sentry must have watched the slow dawn creep over that serrated line of crag and pinnacle during the long years the fort perched on the shaft of Hardknott, 500 feet above the valley of the Esk, was in occupation. Far away to the west a flick of silver tells of the presence of the sea."

Tom Garlick, a schoolteacher who became obsessed with this remote fort, and studied it more intently than most, said: "Hardknott still impresses us with its military efficiency and its wild grandeur. Looking down on it from the Scafell range, it is not difficult to visualise the Roman auxilliarymen on duty here, the rumble of creaking ox wagons up the Pass, or the glint of metal on the parade ground, strange voices and the harsh din of bugles."

Pilgrim's Way

Strolling round the fort will suffice for the average pilgrim who has parked the car in a small area cut into a hillside. William Camden, the Elizabethan antiquary, wrote of the approach to the "castle" being "so steepe and upright that one can hardly ascend up to it." A visitor who wishes to exercise the leg muscles might park the car on the Eskdale side of the pass and walk beside it to the remains of Hardknott Fort. The rising gradient begins near Brotherilkeld (a farm with a Norse name meaning Ulfketil's huts. The name Ulfketil was relatively common until the 14th century).

Hardknott is seen (in good weather) to have a fine view of Eskdale. The fort was to guard the road and was itself impregnable on three sides; a trench was dug to ward off any attacks that might take place from the east.

Pilgrimage 5 – Ninian's Kirk

GR 559299. A 17th century church is called Ninekirks, possibly after St Ninian, an evangelising saint who, early in the fifth century, founded a monastery at Whitburn and is thought to have preached in Cumbria. Approached by footpath from the A66 about 2½ miles from Penrith. Small parking area.

Basic Details

The present church is virtually as it was in 1660 when a Norman church was rebuilt by Lady Anne Clifford. The Norman church had in its turn replaced a Saxon church, in an area where the name St Ninian is venerated. Ninian's original church is said to have been founded between 390 and 400 AD. In the east wall of the chancel is a fragment of inscribed stone dating from the 12th century, when the Normans held sway.

The special features of the present church include an original stone altar, kept under an oak table, also a screen and two canopied box pews. A sanctuary chest, in which church vestments were once kept, has three locks, the keys for which were long since lost.

Ninekirks.

St Ninian

Millward and Robinson (1970) wrote: "The faith of St Ninian helps to strength-en the faith of the historian in the continuity and settlement of the north-west through the Dark Ages."

Historically, he is a shadowy figure, first recorded by the historian Bede some 300 years after his [the saint's] death. It is said that Ninian was born near Solway towards the end of the Roman occupation. He achieved prominence when the kingdom of Rheged took in south-west Scotland and part of Cumbria. Ninian founded a monastery at the Isle of Whithorn in Galloway.

There is a strong belief that St Ninian spent some time in the Penrith area, which in his day might be reached handily by road. Brougham, a crossing point of the Eamont, was quite well populated. Douglas Simpson, in a paper about Brougham (1959), suggested that St Ninian chose as his cell a cave in the red sandstone cliffs of the Eamont. The place where he preached may be that now occupied by Ninekirks.

Pilgrim's Way

Consult OS map The English Lakes (North Eastern Area). Drive eastwards from Penrith along the Roman road, now prosaically known as the A66. At the crossing point of the river Eamont you will see (right) the redstone remains of Brougham Castle.

Beyond a turning-off point for Brougham (right) there is a newish road cutting and on it the so-called Countess Pillar, where Lady Anne Clifford bid what turned out to be a last farewell to her mother before returning to her home in the South. A short distance away (right) is a large building, set back from the road. It is known as Whinfield Park.

At this point, consider pulling off the A66 on the left. There is usually parking space in a small enclosure. Follow the footpath shown on the map. It runs near the Eamont, then descends Church Bank into an 80-acre field, at the centre of which stands Ninekirks. In summer the field might hold a crop of ripening grain. A broad path is left for visitors when services are occasionally held here. There is no heating. When rural electrification was taking place about 1962, the Electricity Board mentioned a figure of £100 as the cost of connecting Ninekirks to the national grid. If the work had not been done then, the cost would have risen to £700. The Rector and churchwardens agreed to the church being connected but the cable goes no farther than an outside wall. The church has never been wired inside.

When you have visited the church, consult your OS map, then follow the path to near Hornby Hall and turn right to return to the point where the walk began.

The Saints Came Marching In...

CELTIC missionary saints of the 5th and 7th centuries, arriving in Cumbria by boat or on foot, left a lasting impression on local life. Some had braved the Irish Sea and others launched their frail craft on the swirling currents of Solway Firth. Yet more had a hard slog through woodland and over hill, through gaps in the Pennine range, to the east of which lay Northumbria, an Anglian kingdom founded, according to tradition, in 547 AD.

Northumbria had arisen through the expansionist zeal of colonists from the seaboard of north-west Europe. Arriving in the muddy reaches of the Humber estuary they claimed land "north of the Humber" with such good effect their territory extended to the Firth of Forth. (Edinburgh would be named after Edwin, an English king). Angles (the first English) were urged by their king to go west, which they did on a broad front, some occupying the fan-shaped valley of the Eden, between Lakeland and the Pennines.

If Cumbria had a special saint, it would surely be St Kentigern, also known as Mungo, who died in 612. Like many another hallowed person of that time, the reality was to become blurred by legend. In medieval literature, details of a saint's life would become so romanticised there would be more legend than hard fact. Yet the spirit of St Kentigern still broods over the northern part of the region, where several churches are named after him.

Kentigern's major exploits were not set down during his lifetime. A biography written by Jocelyn, of Furness Abbey tells a fantastic story in which Kentigern is presented as the son of a woman of royal (Scottish) birth. In about the year 518, she was inspired by the example of Our Lady to retain her virginity. The advances of a chieftain called Ewen were spurned and consequently her father, King Urien, sent her to be a servant on a farm in the Lowlands.

The lustful Ewen followed and seduced her. By the cruel laws of the time, she was condemned to die by being tied to a chariot that was sent rolling backwards down a steep hillside on the Lammermuir range. Both the young lady and her unborn child survived without injuries. The hapless young lady was now proclaimed a witch and condemned to a witch's death by water. Taken to the shore of the Firth of Forth, she was placed in a coracle and set out on an ebb tide without oar or rudder.

The boat was washed upon the farther shore of the Firth, where she gave birth to a boy child. Some shepherds took her to St Sevanus, the local hermit, who christened the mother Thanew and bestowed on the child the unwieldy name of Cyentogern, which became Kentigern through popular usage.

Everybody's Friend

As an evangelising saint, Kentigern was joyously active in Cumbria in the middle of the 6th century – a turbulent time. Local people had lapsed into "ydolatrie". As St Mungo, a name derived from mynghu, meaning "dear friend", he became patron saint of Glasgow. Mungo is a name occurring in Cumbria, as in Mungrisedale, which lies between the A66 and Caldbeck, to the north-east of Keswick.

The church in "Mungo's Dale" is dedicated to him. We can only guess at what stood here in Kentigern's time, but the present structure, of mid-18th century date, is attractive in its simplicity. (In the neighbouring hamlet of Mosedale is a Quaker Meeting House that is open during the summer, when helpers dispense historical information and refreshments).

In about 553 AD, Kentigern visited Caldbeck, where another church is dedicated to him and a riverside well takes on his nickname of Mungo. St Kentigern's Day (January 13) was once commemorated at Caldbeck by a special service. A 15th century missal containing a service for that day, and used locally, is now kept at Ampleforth College in North Yorkshire.

Kentigern at Crosthwaite

The most famous incident in Kentigern's ministry in Cumbria concerns the setting up of a cross in a clearing of a forest at what is now part of Keswick. The holy spot became known as Crosthwaite. The saint would preach in his own tongue – i.e., Welsh – to a congregation said to have been over 500. (This may be the story-teller's ruse of rounding up figures to impress his hearers).

Of this momentous visit, his biographer, wrote: "When he had come to Karleolum, that is Carlisle, he heard that many among the mountains were given to idolatry and ignorant of divine law. Thither he turned aside and God helping him and confirming the word by signs following, he converted to the Christian religion many from a strange belief and others who were erroneous in the faith."

Kentigern is thought to have been heading for Wales but, "turning aside from thence [Crosthwaite] the saint directed his steps to the sea-shore, and through all his journey scattering the seed of divine word, gathered in a plentiful and fertile harvest unto the Lord." In due course, at Crosthwaite, a church of wood and thatch would be built – the humble beginnings of a story that led to the creation of a parish extending through the northern dales of Lakeland, from Skiddaw to Bowfell and Great Gable. (So strong was Kentigern's appeal in Cumbria, he was given the patronage of no less than eight of the big old parishes).

Patron of Patterdale

Did Patrick, the premier saint of Ireland, bestride our quiet hills? According to tradition, he was born, c389 AD, at either Birdoswald or Bewcastle, near Hadrian's Wall, and as a young man was captured by pirates and taken to Ireland.

Here by strength of personality and many good deeds he soon attained sainthood and, as was the way with Celtic saints, was ubiquitous. Patrick was said to have been shipwrecked at Heysham, beside Morecambe Bay and also to have preached in the valley near Ullswater that was to become known as Patterdale, baptising converts at a well overlooking the big lake's southern bay.

The author of a short history of dale and church, available locally, refers to an earlier name, Patricksdale, and conjectures that the saint, having been shipwrecked on Duddon Sands, walked eastwards until, by Ullswater, as related, he baptised local people using a well near the boat landings at Glenridding. I prefer to think of the dale being named, as one historian suggested, after a crusty 10th century Norse landowner called Patraic. The first-known incumbent of the church in Patterdale was Adam Abbott, curate, in 1581. By that time both Patrick and Patraic had been dead for centuries.

The present Patterdale church is Victorian, replacing a plain little chapel that lay in the vast parish administered from Barton, a settlement at the other end of the lake. (Barton church, in its circular churchyard on an artificially-raised mound, close to one of the springs feeding the River Eamont, was surely built on what had been a pagan site).

Holy Women

The life of Bega, a saint revered on and around St Bees Head, which is said to have been named after her, was compiled from legendary accounts published centuries after her death. The main elements were noted in a 13th century manuscript, possibly the work of Everard, Abbot of Holm Cultram (1150-1192), some four centuries after she had gone to her reward – if, indeed, she ever lived!

From a medieval sketch of St Bega.

The manuscript, transcribed in 1842, was said to be an account of the life of Bega (or Bec) along with a list of the miracles performed through her influence. Early in the 7th century, it was written, "a certain very powerful King in Ireland...excelled his predecessor kings in riches and glory." (Was this Donald III, who reigned over Ireland between 612 and 642?). The beauty of his daughter, Bega, became widely known among well-to-do young men, including "the sons of princes and chiefs," some of them living overseas.

Bega, having become a Christian, preferred a reflective life than the lot of a married woman. She would not "contract the bands of marriage with anyone by her own will." Her fame reached the ears of the son of the Norwegian king, a son who was soon to succeed to the throne. Envoys were sent to Ireland to confirm reports of Bega's beauty and, if they were favourable, to ask the king for her hand in marriage. They were beguiled by the young lady. Arrangements for a wedding were put in hand.

Bega, distressed at the prospect of marriage against her will, and keen to serve the Church, had a dream in which she heard a voice. Her prayers would be answered. The speaker added: "Arise, therefore, and take the bracelet by which thou are pledged to me, and descending to the sea thou shalt find a ship ready prepared, which will transport thee unto Britain." Carrying the bracelet as a talisman, she made her way through the sleeping guards to the harbour, where she found a ship and sailed east, eventually reaching the Cumbrian coast.

One story told about St Bega is that on the sea crossing, she was caught in a storm. When the boat was on the point of sinking, she vowed that if God delivered her she would lead a prayerful life. She was spared, landed in Fleswick Bay, an inlet on the red sandstone headland, and visited my Lord of Egremont, asking for a plot of land on which she might build a place of sanctuary. He, scornfully, said he would give her as much land as was covered by snow on the following day, which was Midsummer Day. Astonishingly, snow fell, covering a three-mile stretch of ground around the headland.

No traces of Bega or her monastery are known, but a priory was eventually to appear at St Bees. Here, for many years, was kept a bracelet, the old English name for which is *beag*, a word resembling Bega. Was our pert and attractive little Irish princess none other than a cult figure? One of the witnesses to an early charter of St Bees Priory, which had been founded by William le Meshin in 1125, had the good Gaelic name of Gillebecoc, which means "servant of Bega".

Another Irish lady, St Bridget (or Brigit or Bride), is remembered by the church-folk at Beckermet, where she is the patron saint, also at Bridekirk and Kirkbride, where is to be found a stained glass window with figures of Patrick, Brigit and Columba. Was she another figment of the medieval imagination?

Bridekirk, about three miles north of Cockermouth, has a neo-Norman church (1870) with ancient foundations. The 12th century font is carved, as noted by the antiquarian Collingwood, "with dragons and strange beasts" also a reassessment of the expulsion from Eden and the baptism of Christ. On the fourth side is a portrait of the artist with chisel and mallet and his autograph signature in runes of the 12th century which in modern English mean "Richard me wrought, and to this beauty eagerly me brought."

The Islander

St Cuthbert, who was revered throughout Northumbria, and St Herbert, a friend who chose to live on a small island in Derwentwater, died and were taken up to heaven on the same day.

Virtually all that we know about Herbert is what is recorded in a poem (in Latin) written by a monk of Lindisfarne, plus some references in Bede, who noted: "There was a priest of praiseworthy life named Herebert (sic), who ... lived the life of a hermit on an island in the great lake which is the source of the river Derwent." Herbert's home was a two-roomed cell, half chapel, half house. He ate lake fish for dinner whether or not it was a fast day. There was little else available. His only enemies were said to be winter and rough weather.

The great Diocese of Lindisfarne extended across the northern Pennines and whenever Cuthbert, who had become Bishop, travelled to Carlisle, it was arranged that Herbert would leave his little island to see him, so that he might renew his friendship and seek spiritual advice. In the year 685, noted that great historian Bede, Cuthbert arrived in Carlisle to visit the queen of Ecgfrith, who was campaigning against the Picts. The queen was at the residence of her sister-in-law, the Abbess of Carlisle.

Cuthbert was taken on a sightseeing trip of what remained of the Roman city. He saw a fountain "wondrously constructed by the Romans" and still working over 150 years after their day. Anglian buildings were of wood, not stone. The surviving masonry at Carlisle was regarded as "the cunning work of giants". In 686, Cuthbert was in Carlisle to consecrate priests and give a blessing to the queen, who was now widowed. He and Herbert met, as usual.

An ailing Cuthbert said: "Ask me now about whatever you have in mind, because we shall see each other no more in this life. The time of my death is coming near." In tears, Herbert said: "Pray the Almighty that as we have served Him together on earth, we may pass to heaven at the same time." The prayer was answered. They both died on March 20 in the next year, Herbert on his islet in a lake, Cuthbert on the Inner Farne, surrounded by seals and salt water.

Cuthbert, whose body was found uncorrupted years after the interment, became the centre of a cult.

When there was a threat of increased Viking raids, in 875, the monks reverently bore his carved oak coffin and various ecclesiastical treasures from Lindisfarne. They went from place to place until the saint's bones were given a final resting place at Durham in the year 999 AD. The tomb behind the high altar bears the single word Cuthbertus. Sixteen Cumbrian churches are dedicated to this saint and a well bearing the name of St Cuthbert is to be found at Edenhall, near Penrith.

What of St Herbert? A 14th century Bishop of Carlisle was reading church history when he came across an account of the two saints – St Cuthbert and St Herbert – who had been such close friends 700 years before. The Bishop, noting that they had died on the same day, wrote to the church in Crosthwaite with instructions that a mass should be held every 13th April "ad memoriam Herberti." A spring festival developed. Thus did St Herbert achieve lasting recognition.

William Camden, the Elizabethan topographer, wrote of Herbert that he had lived "an Hermeticall Life." He presumably had no time left to sin. Sir Wilfred Lawson bought the island in 1761 and clear-felled what timber he found, replanting with a Lakeland "mix" – oak, ash, thorn, pine, yew and the alien beech. Hutchinson, in his late 18th century account of Cumberland, wrote: "The remains of Herbert's hermitage appear to this day, one apartment twenty foot long and sixteen broad probably his chapel, the other, narrower, his cell."

Wordsworth, in 1800 wrote a short poem about Herbert, whom he described as "a self-secluded man." It includes the lines:

> *Stranger, not unmoved,*
> *Wilt thou behold this shapeless heap of stones –*
> *The desolate ruins of Saint Herbert's cell.*

The foundations of a small building on the island were not the remains of Herbert's cell but of a chapel frequented by pilgrims. Canon Rawnsley, of Crosthwaite, revived the notion of a medieval pilgrimage to the island when he was vicar of Crosthwaite in the 19th century. He boated out a congregation and preached a sermon. (Herbert is the patron of the modern Roman Catholic church at Windermere).

Early Churches

When, in course of time, a Christian church was being served by a full-time priest, he heard confession, conducted services in Latin and was regarded by local people as "a bulwark against medieval fears of hell and damnation." The priest drew funds from tithes and distributed these among the sick and poor.

Although, at first, steps were taken to abolish pagan practices, it was eventually decided, with the authority of a papal dictum, that earlier beliefs and customs should be Christianised and enfolded in the arms of mother church. Twenty-seven of Cumbria's old churches adopted St Michael as their patron. He was usually summoned where there had been a notable pagan site.

Pilgrimage 6 – Kentigern and Crosthwaite

Great Crosthwaite was one of the big ancient parishes of the Lake District. Crosthwaite Church, which stands rather less than a mile from the centre of Keswick, and is the spiritual home for a much smaller area, stands in a cul de sac, with space for a car to be parked.

Pilgrim's Way

Park the car near the boat landings by Derwentwater and walk the short distance to Friar's Crag, an outstanding viewpoint for Derwentwater and the Borrowdale Fells. The Crag was a point of embarkation for prayerful folk who made the short voyage to St Herbert's island, which is less than a quarter of a mile long and might be seen at the centre of the lake. Everyone who, on April 13, took part in Mass that was celebrated on St Herbert's Island, in memory of Herbert and Cuthbert, was granted a 40-days' indulgence.

Pause before a memorial to the Victorian philosopher, John Ruskin, before leaving Friar's Crag for Keswick, a town that began as a dairy farm, judging by the derivation of its name – kes [cheese] and wic [village]. The impressive range of Victorian buildings beyond Crow Park is known as The Headlands. Almost the whole of Keswick was constructed in Victorian times, when craftsmanship was at its peak. The stimulus for building came from the coming of the railway from Penrith (a railway that was eventually closed; the track-bed from the former station now provides a fascinating walk).

Cross the Greta by a substantial bridge and walk along an impressively straight stretch of road, continuing in the same direction along a cul de sac leading to Crosthwaite Church. As related, it is dedicated to St Kentigern, who raised a cross as a focal point for his preaching. It was written: "Thither he turned aside, and, God helping him...remained some time in a thickly planted place...where he erected a cross as a sign of the faith; whence it took the name, in English, of Crosfeld..."

The present church rests partly on 12th century foundations but has been altered several times, notably in the 14th, 17th and 19th centuries. Look on the interior walls of the church for one of nine consecration crosses, marking the points at which the bishop anointed the walls when the church had been restored in Tudor times. (Twelve consecration crosses were incised on the outside of the building).

A major tourist attraction is a white marble memorial to Robert Southey (1774-1843), a long-time resident of Keswick who in 1813 became Poet Laureate. It was Southey who wrote the famous story of the Three Bears. In the original tale there was no mention of Goldilocks. William Wordsworth composed the epitaph on his memorial. Southey was interred in the churchyard, where the grave is sign-posted.

Pilgrimage 7 – Martin and Martindale

Martindale is one of several dramatic valleys tucked away from the gaze of the world and reached by following a minor road from Pooley Bridge, on the south side of Ullswater. The road to Howtown is narrow, winding and extremely busy during the holiday season. From Howtown there follows the zig-zags of the Hause, lifting the visitor to where St Peter's, a Victorian church, looks incongruous in an area of spectacular fell country. St Martin's Church is almost a mile to the south of this new church.

Basic Details

The present church, a barn-like structure, built of rough stones, dates from the reign of the first Elizabeth (1633) but on the south side, the foundations of an older structure are in view. The nave and chancel are under one sturdy roof. The porch is probably an 18th century addition made when the earthen floor of the church was flagged.

A 14th century stoup for holy-water, with scoring said to have been made when local men needed to sharpened arrowheads, may have been a Roman altar that adorned a wayside shrine on High Street. The churchyard has a yew tree, the age of which has been estimated at 1,300 years.

Until the 19th century, Martindale was a perpetual curacy under Barton. It is related that when Richard Birkett, the first "vicar" died, no one would take on the job because of the poor stipend and so parishioners performed the services by turns. "At length, a little decrepit man called Brownrigg, to whom Mr Birkett had taught a little Latin and Greek, was by the parishioners appointed perpetual reader." The parishioners persuaded the Bishop to grant him deacon's orders. He served the church at Martindale for 48 years.

Until the year 1881, this was the parish church of Martindale. In 1882, the building was stripped of its minstrels' gallery, which once accommodated the choir, whose singing was supported by pitchpipe and bass fiddle.

Pilgrim's Way

Refer to OS map The English Lakes (North Eastern Area). There is a postbus service from Penrith to Martindale. The late morning "steamer" from the pier at Glenridding calls at Howtown pier and energetic pilgrims who use it now have a muscle-tugging walk up the Hause, though the stress of the climb is eased by the zig-zags. Pause now and again to admire the view of Ullswater, the second largest lake in the region, its twisting outline stretching away to the north. On a good day you will see the blue-grey range of the Pennine fells.

On reaching the summit of the Hause, pass the Victorian church and keeping to the left after a mile you will reach Martindale Church. The view has now opened out to reveal the deep glacial trough of Martindale. The main valley resembles a tuning fork, with two prongs, Ramps Gill and Bannerdale. Between them is a shapely fell known as the Nab, the resort of red deer.

Figures Carved in Stone

D R PARKER, a medical man of the 19th century, helped us to unravel a mystery of the stone crosses that were focal points for early Christian witness. He visited Gosforth, where Eskdale meets the Cumbrian Plain. With him was the Rev W S Calverley, who had theorised that there was a pagan link through carvings on the tall, slender, sandstone cross that had stood locally for nine centuries.

A ladder was produced. With typical Victorian flamboyance, Parker instructed his coachman to scrub the head of the cross with brush and water, exposing the ancient carving. Into view, as the cleaning proceeded, came details from an ancient tale dealing with a timeless theme – with the tussle between the forces of good and evil. Studied in finer detail, here was a type of story of which nightmares are made, the gods versus a monster, the double-headed Wolf, offspring of the evil Loki.

How did this pre-Christian story come to be on a cross now standing on consecrated ground? Local history had reached a turning point. Christianity was diffusing heathen ideas by absorbing and Christianising them. Yet the Nordic influence remained strong. Bishop Nicholson of Carlisle detected traces of the old Scandinavian influence in the latter part of the 17th century. To him, the Vikings were "anciently gross Idolaters and Sorcerers." They had "brought Paganism along with them into this Kingdom." They might for some time "practise their Hocus tricks here in the North, where they were most numerous and least disturbed."

With the coming of the Norsefolk, the northern landscape became tenanted by trolls, boggles and the barguest, a spectral hound with eyes as big as saucers. All manner of strange creatures were abroad during the long winter nights. The Norse Loki, who figures on the Gosforth Cross, is the devil in the form of a strange creature, half man, half wolf-demon. (See the so-called hornless devil on a fragment of stone at Kirkby Stephen parish church, in the Upper Eden).

From the earliest times, the Cross was a symbol of the Christian faith. Slivers of wood said to have been part of the original wooden cross on which Christ was crucified were in circulation among the more guillible gentry who had visited the Holy Land. As missionary monks spread the Word through the North, the Cross took on a more durable stone form.

In the mid-7th century, when Anglian settlers arrived in Cumbria from the east, stone crosses became the focal point for preaching by itinerants. One notable cross was raised at Irton. The cross at Gosforth was an artistic as well as religious triumph. Stand before it, even in its worn state, and you sense the triumph of Christ over whatever local gods were being worshipped. Here was a bonding of ancient pagan notions with the Christian faith – a proclamation of the victory of Christ over the heathen beliefs still to be found in the dream-world of ordinary folk.

In the cross, the pagan theme of the Sacred Tree was supplanted by a Christian tree using stone carved in the form of a tree and its foliage. At Gosforth, a Crucifixion scene appears high on the east face. Christ is shown having his side pierced by the spear of a soldier. A second figure may be that of Mary Magdalene.

Wheel-headed crosses and hogback tombstones tell us about the faith of the North settlers who in about the 10th century arrived in Cumbria from Ireland and the Isle of Man. Some would have married red-haired Irish lasses and become converts to Christianity. Those who remembered the high crosses of Ireland would seek to raise similar crosses in their new home. They are almost all to be found at the fringe of the mountainous area.

The so-called Giant's Grave in the churchyard of St Andrew's at Penrith is really a combination of two 10th century Anglo-Viking crosses with hogback tombstones in between. The highest cross, standing at rather more than 11 ft, is decorated with interlace. The other cross, which is only fractionally shorter, still bears a carving of a bound male figure with a serpent above his head. A woman stands nearby. In another part of the Penrith churchyard is a third old cross, this being known as the Giant's Thumb.

Calverley's work on ancient crosses interested a young artist and scholar, W G Collingwood. He had become secretary to John Ruskin, the Victorian philosopher and art critic who spent his later days at Brantwood, a mansion overlooking Coniston Water. Collingwood extended his interest in Anglo-Saxon and Viking studies to take in pre-Norman sculpture.

When Ruskin died, Collingwood provided him with an appropriate memorial, to be seen in the churchyard at Coniston. The grave is marked by a Celtic cross, carved of Tilberthwaite stone, its base set on a piece of rock brought from Elterwater.

Symbolism was widely used in an age when comparatively few people were educated. Retained in the church at Long Marton, in the Eden Valley, are two tympana, believed to be Anglian. A tympanum is a space over a door between the lintel and arch. One of the Edenvale examples bears the impressions of a dragon, a winged ox in a boat and a winged shield, charged with a cross. The other tympanum, over the original west doorway, is carved with dragon, merman, club and cross. There are three lines of chequers in the base.

Pilgrimage 8 – Bewcastle Cross

Bewcastle, also known as Shopford, is a northern outpost of Cumbria, 25 miles north-east of Carlisle, three miles east of the B6318 and a mere seven miles from Scotland. Bewcastle boasts one of the glories of the Anglo-Saxon period in an ancient stone cross which now stands on land once occupied by a Roman fort. It is now the churchyard of St Cuthbert's. Interpretive panels dealing with the famous cross and other aspects of local history are on view locally. The pub, called The Drove, relates to a time when cattle from Scotland were driven on the hoof to the English markets.

Basic Details

Bewcastle Cross stands in the yard of St Cuthbert's Church, which occupies a site used for Christian worship since the latter part of the 8th century. Little if anything of a church of that period remains. The tower was added during extensive alterations in 1792 and more recently in 1901, when some of the more severe modifications of the Georgian period were amended.

Bewcastle's 14ft 6in sandstone shaft is of the late 7th century. "Belted" Will Howard, who wanted William Camden, a visiting antiquary, to view it at close range, removed the headpiece in the 17th century. Subsequently all trace was lost. The cross shows the highest quality of stone carving, the symbols including Christian and animal imagery.

On the east face is a spiral vine motif. The west face has representations (from top to bottom) of what is assumed to be John the Baptist and the Lamb of God, Jesus Christ; and a Prince of Northumbria with a falcon. On other faces is vine-scrolling (a style with an eastern Mediterranean origin) and various birds and beasts.

John Parker (1977) wrote of the Gosforth cross, which commemorates Alcfrith, a son of King Oswy of Northumbria, that "historians who gaze upon the cross's slender beauty...must chew their nails nervously and wonder why it is not safe in some museum." The Cross was described by. R G Collingwood as "perhaps the finest extant masterpiece of Early English stone carving". In more recent times, Niklaus Pevsner, who had also seen the cross at Ruthwell, on the Scottish side of Solway, maintained that there is "nothing as perfect as these two crosses of comparable date in the whole of Europe."

After being vacated by the Romans, at the end of the 4th century, Bewcastle probably became a community of Anglo-Saxons who had been converted to Christianity. It later became the home of a Viking chief called Beauth. Stones from the Roman fort were a handy quarry for a Norman castle, of which little remains.

Pilgrim's Way

Someone called Bewcastle "a parish rather than a place". It is not on a main tourist route but several thousand pilgrims annually visit this last flourish of England, to view the church and the cross. The landscape is open, the horizons are low and the sky is vast.

Hadrian's Wall continues to fire the imagination. The church at Bewcastle stands on a six-acre plot that up to its abandonment by the Romans in 367 AD held a highly-mobile cavalry unit that might collaborate with the troops holding the Wall by attacking an enemy force in the rear as they came up against a frontal barrier.

At Bewcastle, the past tends to intrude on the present. A former Rector lost his vegetable garden. It was decided to extend the graveyard, and such was the archaeological interest of the rest of the area on which the Rectory stands that extension in any other direction was unthinkable.

Pilgrimage 9 – Gosforth Cross

Gosforth, which stands beside the A595, is the "gateway" to majestic Wasdale, in the far west of Lakeland.

Basic Details

Tall and slender, the Gosforth cross has a 15 ft sandstone shaft, surmounted by a small wheelhead of the Celtic ring type. The lower part of the shaft is cylindrical and above the shaft is rectangular.

Each side of the upper part is capped with a symbol of the Trinity. The figures on the sides of the cross have been interpreted as a pictorial representation of the Norse poem Voluspa, which foretells the end of the world, when "the son of the gods, all powerful, who rules all" will come.

The base of another cross survives; it was sawn off in 1789 and made into a sundial. At Gosforth, some hogback tombs of ancient chieftains were incorporated in the foundations of a subsequent Norman church. Inside the church is a hogsback at the end of which is a striking impression of Christ crucified.

Pilgrim's Way

See the Gosforth cross on your way to Wasdale. The cross, of rose-tinted stone, is visible from the road. Then motor on to Wasdale, a name derived from the Norse *vatn*, meaning water, and *dalr*, or valley. Wastwater, which is the deepest in the country, has a maximum depth of 254 ft.

Pilgrimage 10 – Wasdale Church

For most pilgrims, the motor journey is a great experience. The road from Gosforth heads for four miles between shapely hills and offers a view of a trinity of mountains – Great Gable, Yewbarrow and Lingmell – which appear on the emblem of the Lake District National Park. A capacious car park lies a few minutes walk from the little church which has Norse associations.

St Olaf's, Wasdale Head, is in such grand surroundings that Wordsworth wrote of "a temple built by God's own hand – mountains its wall, its gorgeous roof the sky." St Olaf's does not try to compete with nature and is classed among the smallest churches in the land. Externally, the building is just 42 x 16 ft, with walls 6 ft 6 inches high. There is seating for fewer than 50 people.

Piecing together a history of St Olaf's is not easy. The church was at some stage a chapel of rest of St Bees. It had been nameless for 450 years when, in 1977, the Bishop of Carlisle put it under the patronage of St Olaf, recalling the man who converted the Norwegians to Christianity. This was appropriate in an area where some Norse blood still flows in the veins of local people.

Wasdale Head has long been associated with climbers, several who met with accidents being buried in the churchyard. Drawn on a window is the outline of Napes Needle, on Great Gable, which is Lakeland's most famous stack. A man who helped to popularise the local crags for sport wrote that climbing in the Caucasus is safe and easy; in the Alps is often dangerous and, as practised at Wasdale Head, is at once difficult and dangerous.

There is now only one service a month at Wasdale Head. The priest-in-charge, who lives at Gosforth, has the care of two other churches. The Wasdale community is tiny, with but two dozen names on the civil electoral roll. "In the main, the church runs itself," one clergyman told me. "The local people import me to do the liturgical bits and pieces." He summed up the building as "basically a shell, with some very old beams that some say came off a Viking ship. We have no way of verifying that."

Lacking the rights of burial, Wasdale Head lay on the Corpse Track, along which passed coffins holding those who had died in Ennerdale. The Track extended over Black Sail Pass to Wasdale, thence via Burnmoor Tarn to Boot in

55

Eskdale. One of the tales told concerns the coffin of a woman who had a waspish personality now being borne on ponyback from Wasdale Head to St Catherine's in Eskdale. The pony collided with a rowan tree, shaking up the coffin and reviving the "dead" woman. She resumed her old domineering role in the family. When she again died, and the funeral procession was approaching the rowan tree on the moor, the husband said to the man holding the pony: "Tak it easy, lad."

The body of a male member of the Porter family was strapped to the back of a fell pony to be borne across the moor for burial. Mist descended. The pony bolted and both it and the coffin vanished into the mist. The distraught mother of the dead man died of shock. Once again a funeral party set out for Eskdale and once more it was enveloped in mist. Both pony and coffin disappeared. When the mist cleared, a pony was found grazing on the fellside. There was a coffin on its back. It was not that of Mrs Porter but of her son. No trace was ever found of the mother.

Will Ritson, one of the old-time characters of Wasdale, was fond of telling a story about John Wilson (1785-1854) who attended a social evening, known in Lakeland as a Merry Neet: "T'aad Parson was theeer among t'rest. When they'd gitten a bit on, Wilson mead a sang aboot t'parson. He med it reet off t'stick end. He began wi' t'Parson fus, then he got to t'Pope, an' then he turn'd it to th'divil, an' sic like, till he hed 'em fallin' off theer cheers [chairs] wi' fun. Parson was quite stunn'd an' rayder vex't like but ... at last he burst oot laughin' wi' t'rest."

The Monastic Influence

Cartmel Priory.

WHEN, in 1086, William the Conqueror ordered a great "description" or survey of England, most of Cumbria was not mentioned, being within the kingdom of Scotland. Then in 1092, William II extended Norman rule to Carlisle, driving out Dolfin, the Scottish ruler and colonising the area with his followers, including English peasants, who arrived with their families and livestock.

William divided his new territory between Ranulph de Meschines, who became lord of the lands from Solway to Derwent, and Ivo de Tailboism, Baron of Kendal. By 1112, the Vipont or Veteripont family were the principal landowners at Appleby, in the Eden Valley, where an imposing castle appeared.

The position of other castles marked the strategic importance of the Eden Valley in relation to Scotland. These were built at Carlisle, Brougham and Brough. In addition, stone-built pele towers gave local families and their farm stock a safe shelter until the besiegers, wearied of waiting, moved elsewhere. If the besiegers peevishly put a torch to other buildings, made of wattle-and-daub, with thatched roofs, these could be easily and cheaply replaced.

The Normans preferred to use stone rather than wood. Their castles and parish churches were built durably. No less than 60 churches in Cumbria have some Norman work in their fabric.

The Norman lords, having secured their position in this world gave some thought to their status in the Hereafter by making generous gifts of property and money to the monastic orders. The grateful monks undertook to remember the donors and their families in the prayer life of the abbeys and priories. In some cases, advance arrangements were made for a donor, his nearest and dearest, to be buried within the abbey walls.

Buildings that Impressed

So it was that the Norman abbey rather than Norman secular government played a major part in the life of Lakeland. The monks of 12th century Cumbria engaged in grandiose building schemes. The native folk would stare with drooping lower jaws at immense walls and heavy vaulting. The style fell short of full Gothic style, with its fine detail, simply because the Cistercians were plain folk with plain tastes.

Monks were well-regarded by the medieval peasantry because of their closeness to God and the hospitality they extended to travellers and the poor. In the 13th century, the friars were engaged in robust evangelism. Lacking interest in wordly possessions, they performed good works in local communities.

Three monastic orders – Cistercians, Augustinians and Premonstratensians, or white canons – were to be associated with the Lake District and its environs. The red sandstone ringing the Lake District proved to be a handy source of stone, being easily worked. Cistercians, a comparatively new order, thrived in the north-country and were noted for their intensity at prayer and work. Furness Abbey, in the Vale of the Deadly Nightshade, near modern Barrow, was situated in an area where the sandstone naturally outcropped.

The influence of the big abbeys spread into the Lake District, where there were sheep on the hills, cattle ranches in the dales, bloomeries for iron-smelting and watermills to grind corn. All thrived under the (usually) benign gaze of Norman landowners. Outlying estates were linked to the parent abbey by waymarked tracks and a system of granges.

The hardy little sheep belonging to Furness were named *herdwycks* after the places in which they were kept. They retain the name to this day. Furness, one of the wealthiest Cistercian houses in the North Country, had a splendid grange at Hawkshead that attained such importance a courthouse was added. Furness held the land between Windermere and Coniston Water, also upper Eskdale (the land secure behind a drystone wall) and half of Borrowdale.

The Yorkshire abbey of Fountains had the other half and also Watendlath and Derwent Island. The abbey of Furness had one foot in Yorkshire, with property based on granges at Newby, in the shadow of Ingleborough, and the upper valley of the Ribble.

Shap was the only Lakeland abbey to have a truly fell-country setting. Thomas Gospatrick was its founder and the land was taken over by Premonstratensian canons. Despite its bleak upland situation, Shap had land adequate for 60 cows, 20 mares, 500 sheep with their young until the age of three and for five yoke of oxen. The mares ran in woodland that yielded timber for hedging and to keep the home fires burning.

Cartmel and Conishead lay near the Sands route across Morecambe Bay, a route avoiding the rigours of overland travel. They were in what at one time must have seemed the most isolated part of the kingdom. By the year 1200, the region had shrines for the consolation of travellers, those between Kendal and Windermere making a special effort to visit the Shrine of Our Lady set up on an island in Windermere.

Dissolution

All was not sweetness and light. In the 14th century, the Scots were troublesome. Carlisle, Penrith and Appleby were vulnerable to their raids. Furness Abbey was under attack in 1316 and again in 1322 when Robert Bruce was here, later crossing Morecambe Bay at low tide to devastate Lancaster.

Then came Dissolution – "the Great Northern Tragedy" – when Henry VIII brought about the closure of Monasteries that had acquired about a fifth of the best land in England. To the average Laker, the affairs of State were of little concern. To reach London from, say, Kendal, demanded a week of hard travel. What mattered most in the Lakeland parishes was the will of the notable families, such as the Dacres and the Cliffords. The Northerner had a conservative streak, having a regard for the Old Faith and a soft spot in his heart for the monasteries.

The monks had managed their estates wisely and provided employment for many people in a region where the climate was indifferent and the neighbouring Scots were troublesome. In 1536, royal decrees about Dissolution sparked off a north-country rebellion that became known as the Pilgrimage of Grace. It was a protest against King Henry's centralising tendencies and the new religious policy. There was doubtless wry comment at Kendal that the king had selected for his new wife Katharine Parr (1513-1548), the daughter of Sir Thomas Parr, who presided over Kendal Castle.

The Pilgrimage of Grace began to the east of the Pennines with the mustering of 30,000 pilgrims. Its effect to the west of the hill range was less dramatic. At Kirkby Stephen, Robert Thompson, the vicar of Brough, led the rebellion. Companies of men from the surrounding

Katherine Parr.

villages joined those in town and they marched to Penrith, where they joined Sir Edward Musgrave and the men of Edenhall.

In a matter of days, Sir Edward headed an army some 15,000 strong. These pilgrims lacked a determined leader, for almost all the leading families remaining aloof. The small army of Cumbrians dispersed. When tempers rose in South Westmorland, and men marched from Kendal to Lancaster, nothing of significance was achieved and the uprising fizzled out..

Dissolution came when some Cumbrian monasteries were in the process of expansion. The monks of Shap were glorying in their fine west tower. There began a process of stripping the monasteries of saleable items. Cumbrians were hustled into the uncertainties of a new age. Old men recalled a time when the local abbey provided stability and work.

Pilgrimage 11 – Shap Abbey

GR 548153. English Heritage. Lies off the road between Shap and Bampton, on a popular approach to Haweswater. Notice a by-road (left) to Keld. Visit this secluded hamlet to see Keld chapel, small and austere. A notice on the door gives details of where the key may be obtained. Back on the Bampton road, a mile from Shap is a sign directing you to the abbey. A well-surfaced track descends into a secluded valley drained by the River Lowther.

Basic Details

The grand tower of Shap Abbey, added early in the 16th century, is the first monastic feature to come into view as you approach the remains of Westmorland's only abbey, which was established in 1201. Little else remains, the stones having been transported to the village in the 17th century to form a market hall. Walk around and you will see a few stones of the monastic home farm and a watermill. Shap produced a notable churchman, Abbot Richard Redman, who served in the 15th century and went on to become bishop of St Asaph in Wales, followed by Exeter and Ely.

Pilgrim's Way

Refer to the OS Map (English Lakes: North Eastern area). Park the car at Shap without difficulty and, referring to the your map, select a route from a choice of field paths from the village to Shap Abbey, via Keld. The final stretch of path will begin not far from the chapel and traverse high ground above the River Lowther. A return to Shap is possible from the Abbey Bridge and beside the road, entering Shap at the northern end.

Pilgrimage 12 – Furness Abbey

Maintained by English Heritage, a substantial part of the old abbey, once the second richest Cistercian house in England, exists in a secluded vale just off the A590 at the eastern approach to Barrow-in-Furness. The site is "open to view" except at Christmas and on January 1st. Car parking is available.

Furness Abbey.

Basic Details

Furness Abbey (1127-1536) rose in splendour in a quiet valley and the remains of monastic buildings are considerable. Stephen, later king of England, granted the site to the Savigny order, which 20 years later, in 1147, merged with the Cistercians. Wool was the basis of a lucrative trade with Continental merchants.

The monks had fishing rights in the estuaries leading into Morecambe Bay and also in Windermere and Coniston Water. Produce was exported from their busy harbour at Piel. It is suspected that duty was not paid on all the goods subjected to it when it was shipped into Piel.

John Stell, a monk at the time of Henry VI, put his thoughts about the Abbey into verse, in Latin, a translation being:

> *This valley formerly took his name from the herb*
> *Bekan [deadly nightshade] which flourished there,*
> *A sweet place now but then bitter;*
> *Whence the name of the house, Bakensgill, was famous of old.*

Outpost at Hawkshead

Furness had territorial claims at Hawkshead, an area notable for its natural assets – wood for charcoal burning and iron ore to be smelted and used for forgings. A range of buildings included quarters for visiting dignitaries and manorial courts. At Hawkshead, contrary to their rule, the monks had a hunting ground.

The monastic gatehouse, which is all that remains, is simply constructed of rough rubble masonry, but even at a casual glance it would be difficult to mistake this building for a barn. Crow-stepped gables and traceried windows captivate the eye. These, together with the dressings of arched passageway and sculptured niche, are in red sandstone.

Some of the present structure dates from early in the 13th century but most of the gatehouse is 200 years younger. Ann Radcliffe (1794), beholding the gatehouse, mentally conjured up a picture of "the midnight procession of monks, clothed in white and bearing lighted tapers."

Pilgrim's Way

After following the A590 to Barrow, divert at Newby Bridge and drive beside the Leven to Backbarrow, from here returning to the major road. This allows you to sample the atmosphere of one of the best-wooded areas in England. Under Furness Abbey, woodland industries flourished. Large areas were clear-felled in rotation, while still young, and the wood systematically incinerated for charcoal, which was used for the smelting of iron ore.

To arrive by car is too sudden a transition from the modern world to that quieter, more reflective age of the big abbey. Leave the car at a distance and, as Molly Lefebure wrote, "foot-slog into Bekangesgill; feeling more and more of a medieval pilgrim every moment."

Pilgrimage 13 – Cartmel Priory

Cartmel is approached through Grange-over-Sands or from the A590 at High Newton, between Lindale and Newby Bridge.

Basic Details

Cartmel was so isolated there were traces of the most ancient races here for a longer spell than anywhere else. Two kings influenced the development of Cartmel by their desire to pacify the country, to make it habitable and evangelise it for Christianity. At the end of the 7th century, the King of Northumbria gave the lands of Cartmel, "with all the Britons in it", to St Cuthbert, Bishop of Lindisfarne.

In the reign of King John, William Marshall, Baron of Cartmel (afterwards second Earl of Pembroke) founded the Priory Church of St Mary and St Michael, Cartmel. He endowed it with the Manor and all the lands in the district of Cartmel and also certain lands in Ireland. The monks were Canons Regular of St Augustine, who had previously used an old chapel at the seashore.

A romantic tale is told of how the Augustinians chose the site. They found what they thought to be a suitable place and began to dig the foundations. One evening, a mysterious voice told them they were to build instead where there was a valley with two rivers, one flowing north and one flowing south. The church should be built between them. The place was found after much trouble. It was not far from their original site.

Remote and Isolated

Up to the time of the Romantic Movement – roughly the middle of the 18th century – the Cartmel area was probably the most isolated part of England. Look at the map, and you'll see that to the north are the great hills of Lakeland. West and east are the estuaries of Kent and Leven. Where travellers took to the sands, the Kent is seven miles and Leven four miles wide.

Cartmel was therefore an ideal area for monastic settlement being remote and almost surrounded by water. The "land of Cartmel", jutting into Morecambe Bay, is flanked by two lively rivers, the Leven and Winster. In addition, a curious little

Section of a map from Thomas West's Guide (1778).

river known as the Eea, which is Old English for water, rises on Newton Fell and flows down a sweet and sour valley, with limestone to the east and slates to the west. The Eea eventually forms a loop around the Priory.

The founder ordained that Cartmel should be free from subjection to any other religious house. An altar was to be provided with a priest for the people, most of whom tilled the land or went on to the Sands at low tide for shellfish, shrimps and small fish. Not much happened in monastic times. Priors came and went. The canons lived their deeply spiritual lives, helping the people, cultivating the land. The Prior and Canons of Cartmel were responsible for maintaining a guide (Carter) for the Kent Estuary.

About 1316 and 1322, damage was inflicted by Scottish marauders. The canons undertook building projects, extending the central tower diagonally which, in theory, was impracticable and should have collapsed years ago. In practice, it has stood since 1410.

Carved on one of the misericords, those brackets on the choir stalls on which a monk might loll during the long services, is a mermaid with two tails and the obligatory comb and mirror. How was it that such a seductive creature should appear in a religious setting? She represents the lusts of the flesh that the monks should avoid at all costs, as indicated by the outline of a fish (symbol of Christianity) which is swimming away from her.

Dissolution

At the Dissolution, in 1537, an official valuation assessed Cartmel at £91.6.3d. All monasteries under £200 were confiscated by act of Parliament in 1536. Cartmel secured a fresh survey. The valuation was raised to £212.12.10 but it failed to avert dissolution. In 1537, the king's commissioners sent Thomas Holcroft as their agent to turn out the monks and strip the monastery and Priory of its valuables. Lead taken from the roof was valuable for its high silver content.

The minor condition by the founder that an altar should be provided with a priest for the people became a means of preserving the church in its present magnificent state. The law was for the dissolution of monasteries, not parish churches, and so the people claimed a parochial right and the south aisle, which was known as the Town Choir, continued to be used as a church.

In 1620, George Preston of Holker organised the restoration of the Priory and gave considerable financial help. The levying of a rate produced £26. Mr Preston presented the Priory church with oak screen and canopies of the choir stalls and misericords that had survived the 80 years during which the building had been roofless.

From the 18th century, Cartmel became a "stepping stone" used by students of romantic beauty, from Gilpin to Wordsworth and his contemporaries. Visitors during the first half of the last century could not help but notice the shabby state into which the Priory had fallen. In 1859, the 7th Duke of Devonshire, of Holker Hall, paid for the re-roofing of the chancel and the cleaning of the walls. By 1870, the parishioners – inspired by that work – had raised enough to complete the re-roofing and to provide new seating.

At the time of the Dissolution, the monastic buildings were used as a quarry, a source of dressed stone. Little remains of the monastic buildings with the exception of the Gatehouse, which dominates the square at Cartmel. One of the most notable stained glass windows in the church at Bowness-on-Windermere, believed to have been obtained from Cartmel Priory, features an effigy of "Willm Plo...P'or of Kyrkmel" and close by is a picture of several Cartmel monks. From the mouth of one of them issues a label on which is the still legible inscription "William Baraye" or Barrow.

The Barrow family was well represented in the township of Cartmel, occupying among other notable properties Abbot Hall, which stands beside the Bay at Kent's Bank.

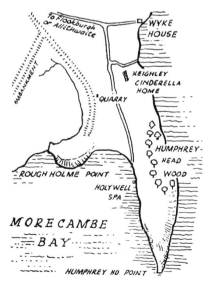

In 1921, some four centuries after the Dissolution, Canonesses of St Augustine came into resident at Boarbank Hall, at Allithwaite. Joseph Bliss had offered the hall for sale. Providentially, land which had been given to St Cuthbert and which was afterwards cultivated by Augustinians of Cartmel for centuries, once again passed into the ownership of the order.

On the lee side of Humphrey Head is the Holy Well of St Agnes. Here, where the slopes are yellowed in spring by primroses and cowslips and where there is an azure haze from bluebells in the coppice woods, was land belonging to Cartmel Priory. In the late 18th and 19th centuries, Humphrey Head had considerable renown with local folk and also visitors from Lancashire. A local man told me: "T'watter's not so good to take at first. It's brakky. I've drunk gallons of it. I heard of one man who drank 26 pints at one go."

The use of the word "brakky" was interesting. Thomas West, who compiled *The Antiquities of Furness* in 1805, referred to this "brakky" taste. He added that the well was "much frequented every summer, and found to be a good remedy for worms..." The water was bottled for distribution over a wide area, some of it being taken regularly to the lead-miners of Alston.

Milk kits containing the water were sent by rail to Morecambe, where an enterprising firm sold it to holidaymakers.

Pilgrim's Way

Walk to Cartmel from Grange-over-Sands. The name grange refers to a granary and was possibly connected with Furness, not Cartmel. Inquire at the Information Centre for details of the walk to Cartmel via Hampsfell, where there is a shelter and a spectacular viewpoint. Or ask about the route through the Fell End golf course and on to Cartmel.

Pilgrimage 14 – Conishead Priory and Chapel Island

The Priory stands in parkland by the coast road to the west of Ulverston. The grounds are open daily and the huge house, which is run by a Buddhist religious trust, is open at prescribed times.

Basic Details

The present building is vast and in the gothic style beloved by the Victorians. The original Priory was founded by William de Tallebois of Lancaster, Baron of Kendal, who gave it to the Canons Regular of St Augustine, an order who had a special regard for the old, the sick and the poor. They had the advowson of St Leonard's Hospital for Lepers at Kirkby Lonsdale.

On the site of the 12th century priory appeared a house built by Gamel de Pennington. The topographer West (1778) described the house as "wonderfully pretty". He mentioned that "the south front is in the modern taste, extended by an arcade. The north is in the gothic stile [sic], with a piazza and wings... The variety of cuminated grounds and winding slopes, comprehended within this sweet spot, furnishes all the advantage of mountains and vales, wood and water..."

A Stepping Stone

When the Braddyll family bought the estate, the present palatial house was constructed (1821-1836). A path runs through woodland to the edge of the Leven estuary, from which rises little Chapel Island, once a "stepping stone" on the low-tide crossing of the Leven. Wordsworth wrote:

> *Upon a small*
> *And rocky island near, a fragment stood*
> *(Itself like a sea rock) the low remains*
> *(With shells encrusted, dark with briny weeds)*
> *Of a dilapidated structure, once*
> *A Romish chapel, where the vested priest*
> *Said matins at the hour that suited those*
> *Who crossed the sands at ebb of morning tide.*

Like the Kent, the Leven has a Sands Guide, whose home is at the edge of the estuary near Ulverston. Another affinity with the Kent is that the Leven is forever changing its course. When it is inshore and on hard ground, the Guide traditionally marked the best route by pushing small branches called "brobs" into the ground.

No one should cross to Chapel Island without an official guide. The tide has to have been on the ebb for six hours before it is safe to cross and the average time from the Ulverston shore to Flookburgh Sandgate is rather less than two hours. Soft spots are most likely to occur when there has been a good deal of rain, swelling the Leven and a beck that runs out of Cark. The beck must be forded.

On Chapel Island, a haunt of rabbits, stood St Catherine's Chapel. The ruins to be seen near the north end of the island do not relate to the monastic building. They were an attempt at reconstruction made by Colonel Braddyll and the time he was rebuilding his mansion.

Pilgrim's Way

Having visited the house, sample the atmosphere of the estate along one of the prescribed paths. If you are lucky, you may be able to join a party going to Chapel Island. On no account make the trip without expert local guidance.

Edwin Waugh, the Lancashire humorist, recorded in his book *Over Sands to the Lakes* (1882) the utterance of one of the official guides who had been asked if any of his colleagues had been lost on the Sands. The guide replied: "I never knew any lost...there's one or two drowned now and then; but they're generally found somewhere I'th bed when th'tide goes out."

The Nonconformists

Friends Meeting House.

IN THE summer of 1652, George Fox, a weaver's son from Leicestershire, having wandered far, with little hope in what he saw of organised religion, arrived in Lancashire. Fox, "moved of the Lord", climbed Pendle, the whaleback hill that is not quite a mountain but which, by its isolation, dominates the landscape for many miles.

The wanderer confided in his *Journal* that "atop a hill I was moved to sound the day of the Lord, and the Lord let me see atop of the hill in what places he had great people to be gathered." These were the folk of widely scattered farms and small villages in Furness and Lunesdale who, being "seekers after truth", were sympathetic to his outlook. Wilfrid Allott, a Quaker historian, was to call them "the great power of the age."

Thus came into being the Religious Society of Friends or the Quakers. George Fox's message – that God's love is available to all, wherever they might be – had such an appeal that by 1690 the number of Friends had risen to about 50,000. A highpoint in the Quaker story had occurred on Trinity Sunday, June, 1652, when, at a rock outcrop on Firbank Fell, Fox preached to an estimated 1,000 people. His outdoor rallying point was to be subsequently known as Fox's Pulpit.

Prior to that event he had been at Sedbergh, preaching in the churchyard to "priests and professors and farming folk from many miles around." The last-named were attending the Whitsun Wednesday Fair, a time for the hiring of farm servants. In the words of his *Journal:* "The next First Day I came to Firbank Chapel in Westmorland, where Francis Howgill and John Audland had been preaching in the morning. John Blaykling came. While others had gone to dinner I went to a brook and got a little water, and then sat on top of a rock.

"In the afternoon people gathered about me. Above a thousand for three hours. Many old people went into the Chapel and looked out of the window thinking it strange to see a man preach on a hill, and not in their Chapel." Fox parried their comments with the words: "I was made to open to the people that the steeplehouse and that ground on which it stood were no more holy than the mountain."

Fox – the man in the leathern breeches – mounted his horse and cantered away (but not for long), leaving behind many thoughtful people. The Victoria County History of Cumberland describes his power in these words: "The religious instincts of the people began to gravitate towards Fox, who in a few years was almost universally accepted as the sovereign pontiff of Cumberland. The Puritan preachers were so utterly forsaken, the Churches in some parishes stood empty."

At Home in Furness

The first Quakers met in private houses, barns and even in graveyards. Margaret, widow of Judge Thomas Fell, of Swarthmoor Hall, near Ulverston, suffered four and a half years of imprisonment in Lancaster Castle because she refused to discontinue the use of her home as a Quaker place of worship. George Fox, who had first visited Swarthmoor in 1652, persuaded the Judge and his family of his religious integrity. The Judge offered Fox protection at a time of legal intolerance in religious matters. When the Judge died, Fox married his widow and they lived at Swarthmoor Hall. Some of his possessions are held here.

Thomas Pennant peevishly recorded (1774): "In after-time the melancholy

A segment of the Castlerigg Stone Circle near Keswick.
An additional 10 stones form a rectangle at the south side. Castlerigg is not a true circle, the diameter varying from 100 to 110 feet. Originally there were 50 stones, a number that has been much reduced.

Long Meg stands apart from her brood of "Daughters"
on level ground between the Pennines
and the Lakeland fells.

Above: Walkers about to set off across low-tide Morecambe Bay.

Below: The Friends' Meeting House at Brigflatts near Sedbergh.

Above: Josephina Banner, the sculptress, in her home-cum-studio. Some of her
work is to be found in Lakeland churches and the Priory at Cartmel.
Below: A tapestry in Patterdale Church.

Above: One of the stone bears in the yard at Dacre Church.
Below: Memorial to railway-builders at Outhgill, Mallerstang.

Left: William Wordsworth, the best-known Lakeland poet. The portrait is from a Daguerreotype.

Right: A "boon day" at Ninekirks, near Brougham. The church is virtually as it was when Lady Anne Clifford re-built it in the 17th century.

Above: Matterdale Church.
Below: A Victorian print of Wythburn, between Thirlmere and Helvellyn.

Cartmel Priory, on a peninsula washed by Kent, Leven and the
tides of Morecambe Bay. Notice the diagonal extension
to the central tower.

spirit of *George Fox*, the founder of quakerism, took possession of *Swartz-moor* hall, first captivating, with grunts and groans, the kind heart of a widow, the then inhabitant, moving her congenial soul to resign herself to him. From thence this spiritual Quixote sallied out, and disturbed mankind with all the extravagancies that enthusiasm could invent."

By 1689, the Toleration Act having been passed, Friends were free to build their own meeting houses and worship as they chose. A Friends Meeting House is not, like a church, a consecrated building. It is sanctified only by the use to which it has been put. The Society of Friends, steadfast in its religious outlook, began to gain an influence far greater than its numbers might imply.

In Lakeland, Quakers owned most of Colthouse, near Hawkshead, in the Lancashire segment of the Lake District. In 1658, a burial ground was opened near the junction of the Colthouse and Sawrey roads – a junction that became known as Sepulchre Corner. A Meeting Place, a plain building, not at all like a church or chapel, was built in 1688 on a tract of land known as Benson Orchard. The heavy oak door has an enormous lock and key. (Beatrix Potter, a Unitarian, who lived at Near Sawrey, occasionally attended Meeting here).

At Swarthmoor, the porched Meeting House, typical of the early period, "of endearing simplicity", was built close to the Hall and was a gift from George Fox, who had married Judge Fell's widow some 20 years earlier. The initials GF and the date are incised on the lintel over the entrance. George and Margaret Fox were the donors of two chairs and a Bible. A stepped dias known as the Minister's Gallery, was devised for the use of elders, overseers and recorded ministers, the last-named being a feature of early Quakerism. The dias, which is in no way a pulpit, extends across the end of the room and has a capacity of 20 or more people. The main room is separated from the smaller or women's meeting room by a lobby, over both of which was another room, sometimes used as a gallery.

All these rooms and the lobby might be made into one large room for special meetings by the adjustment of movable partitions. One building must serve several sizes of congregation, not only on Sunday (First Day, to use the old Quaker term) but for monthly and quarterly meetings of the group. In the early days women had their own business meeting in a separate room.

Independency

The Act of Uniformity enforced the use of the Book of Common Prayer in every Church in England and parsons were required to give their assent to all that it contained. On St Bartholomew's Day, Sunday, August 24, l662, about 2,000 English clergymen who refused to conform to the doctrine contained therein were driven from their churches in what became known as The Great Ejectment.

Among the displaced parsons was the Rev Christopher Jackson, of Crosby Garrett. Aged only thirty, this graduate of Cambridge travelled to Ravenstonedale, some five miles from Crosby Garrett, where he had a little property. Thomas Dodgson, the Vicar of Ravenstonedale, sympathised with Presbyterianism but had not left the church.

Jackson married Anne Taylor, a local woman. He was the subject of much humour because of his threadbare clothes. When one of the local clergy mentioned this to his face, he replied: "If my coat is bare, it is not turned." He was none the less respected for his piety and holiness. There is no record locally of where or when he died.

At Ravenstonedale, in 1662, was built the first Nonconformist chapel in Westmorland. This was replaced in 1727 by what became known as the High Chapel to distinguish it from the nearby Methodist chapel, which stood further down the hill. Until 1867, the High Chapel had oak pews capable of seating 200 people and a handsome three-decker pulpit.

Methodism

The Methodist preachers and evangelists who, early in 18th century, spread the Good News in Furness, Hawkshead, Gosforth and other centres, received much help from the Quakers. Their own pioneering work had been conducted 100 or so years before.

John Wesley made the first of many visits to Lakeland in 1751, noting in his diary, "the next day we rode to Ambleside, and on Saturday, 13, over more than Welsh mountains to Whitehaven." In 1759, he was back, visiting the colliers of

Whitehaven and then preaching in the Vale of Lorton, near Cockermouth. People who heard him "found God to be a God both of the hills and valleys, and no where more present than in the mountains of Cumberland." Wesley was no great lover of hills and was implying that God might be found even in Lorton, where one might least expect to find evidence of His great mercy.

An alternative approach to Whitehaven was across Morecambe Bay at low tide. Reading Wesley's Journal of such an expedition, one senses the frustration of a man in a hurry as he waits for the tide to ebb so that he might continue his journey. Wesley was 85 years old when he paid his last visit to Kendal in 1788.

In the early days of Methodism, converts met in their own homes. "Class meetings" were organised for prayer and Bible study. The appeal was largely to the working class folk towards whom the Established Church paid little regard. It is related at Kendal that a man who joined the Methodist cause told his class leader, during a meeting, the "people say I'm cracked." The class leader promptly said: "Let us pray. Oh, Lord, crack a few more – there's plenty of work for them to do down here!"

The home meetings were the nucleus of many Methodist societies that continued to touch the lives of common people through evangelical zeal. The educational side of Methodist was evidenced by both Sunday and day schools. Encouragement was given for members to undertake higher education and to organise business projects.

Methodists, unlike the Anglican church, was not largely dependent upon paid ministers. Methodism thrived through the work and witness of dedicated layfolk, some of whom became local (as opposed to itinerant) preachers. Long before women were admitted to the priesthood, Methodism was making use of their services as preachers.

Methodists forced change on the anachronistic Church of England and reached a peak of achievement early in the 19th century when central Lakeland was opened up both to visitors and new settlers by the coming of the railway to Birthwaite, which was re-named Windermere. Some impressive Methodist chapels were built in the fast-growing communities of Windermere and Ambleside.

To chronicle the story of every Lakeland chapel and of the various strands of Methodism which came together when unity was achieved in the 1930s would be a lifelong task. Two churches worthy of mention are the large complex in Stricklandgate, Kendal, and tiny Hawkshead chapel, tucked away in a corner of one of the squares at Hawkshead. This is a place where visitors might go for quiet prayer or to join in the weekly worship.

Keswick Convention

For one week in July each year, Keswick is given over to the "Conventioners". The Keswick Convention, evangelical in tone, and held in huge tents, was devised by Canon T D Harford Battersby, a dignified, handsome man who had visited the Lake District as an undergraduate and who became a curate to Frederick Myers, Vicar of Keswick, in 1849. When Myers died at an early age, in 1851, Battersby succeeded him as Vicar.

Battersby was much influenced by attending the Oxford Convention. He used the idea for a series of religious gatherings at Keswick. In 1875, he called together 200 people to begin an inter-denominational crusade with the object of strengthening the influence of religion. A tent was erected. The banner above the tent bore words suggested by Robert Wilson, a Quaker of Brigham – "All One in Christ Jesus."

At the 1876 event, "excessive rain, with thunder and lightning, and violent storms of wind" made the tent collapse on the third night, but Robert Wilson and his helpers by the next morning had notices posted up advising people of alternative halls now available to them. Robert Wilson survived Canon Battersby by 22 years; he died in 1905.

One of the genuinely thrilling moments of the week was when young men and women decided to become missionaries abroad, electing publicly to do so at a special meeting. The original tent was soon too small for those attending and was replaced by one capable of taking 4,000 people.

Pilgrimage 15 – Quakers at Brigflatts

Brigflatts, just south of Sedbergh, stands beside a lane leading from the A683. This is the oldest Meeting House in northern England and the second oldest in the land.

Basic Details

Low Brigflatts, by the river Rawthey, was a small village of flax-weavers. Their wooden homes were thatched, contrasting greatly with the stone used in building the Meeting House. This was done as a co-operative enterprise on a plot of land that cost the Friends 10s. Ten shillings also secured land for a burial ground and the first interment was in 1657.

When Brigflatts was open for worship, Friends sat on benches one plank wide and without backs. The building had no proper floor or ceiling and two Friends undertook to stuff the holes with moss. Draughts and damp were endured for 40 years but in 1715 a ceiling was made. A wooden gallery was added, also a pen for dogs. A staircase inside the meeting room reaches the upper room and also gives access to a raised gallery round two sides, as distinct from the minister's gallery.

David Boulton (1998) wrote: "The result was and is a perfect monument to plain, no-nonsense Quaker simplicity. No-one thought to make it beautiful, but its simplicity and functionality are its beauty."

Membership of the meeting fell away for a variety of reasons. The former large population of farmers, farm workers and flax-weavers had declined. There had been a change in the religious climate and other Nonconformist denominations – notably Methodism – were on the ascendant. An inhibiting factor with regard to membership was that for some time Friends who married non-Friends were disowned. Yet Brigflatts is still a spiritual power house and a place of peacefulness and beauty for many wayfarers.

Pilgrimage 16 – High Chapel at Ravenstonedale

Ravenstonedale, near the headwaters of the River Lune, lies just off the major roads, which is part of its appeal. The village may be approached from either the A685, between Tebay and Kirkby Stephen, or from the A683, Sedbergh-Kirkby Stephen.

Basic Details

First visit the parish church, where there is a three-decker pulpit and the pews are set College-style, with rows facing each other across the width of the building. Now inquire about the High Chapel, on the outer wall of which is a large white marble tablet on which is a summary of its history:

"To the Glory of God. This chapel was built and partly endowed by Philip, fourth Lord Wharton, lord of the manor and others, for a congregation of Protestant Dissenters worshipping in a licensed house near this site in the latter part of the 17th century..."

High Chapel, Ravenstonedale.

Lord Wharton

It was said of Philip, 4th Lord Wharton, the most famous Presbyterian Dissenter in the area: "His doors stood open to the outcast ministers of the Word of God, affording them hospitality and refuge." He became known as "the Good Lord", having set up a Bible Trust and becoming a pioneer of religious education.

When the first batch of 1,050 Bibles were distributed, Lord Wharton himself decided on their destination. When he and his fellow trustees died, vacancies on the Trust were filled by co-options until eventually all were of the Anglican persuasion. Towards the end of last century, this situation was vigorously challenged and the High Court of Justice produced a more balanced scheme that still operates.

86

The body of nine trustees would be made up of five Anglicans and four Nonconformists. Half of the income would go for the provision of Bibles for applications within the Anglican Church and the other half from Nonconformist applications. Candidates must be bona-fide scholars, or teachers, of a Sunday School or a member of a young people's society connected with a religious organisation. Certain passages from the Bible must be committed to memory.

Pilgrim's Way

Have a spell away-from-it-all by inquiring at Ravenstonedale about the approach to the deserted railtrack, which may be followed through several flower-decked miles into Smardale, a nature reserve of the Cumbrian Wildlife Trust, in a steep and wooded valley. It is a haunt of red squirrels and, in late summer, the uncommon Scotch Argus butterfly.

The railtrack gives firm, dry walking conditions and has a spectacular stretch at a restored railway viaduct.

Pilgrimage 17 – Hawkshead Church and Chapel

Wordsworth went to school at Hawkshead and it was a place well-known to Beatrix Potter, who lived at Near Sawrey. Her husband was a partner in a firm of solicitors. The premises where he worked are owned by the National Trust and are "open to view".

The Parish Church

The building seen today is dedicated to St Michael and All Angels, succeeding an earlier building. Notice the smooth plaster finish to the stonework. Wordsworth knew Hawkshead well, spending his early schooldays here. He was impressed by the Church on its mound, comparing the "snow-white" building with a throned lady "sending out a gracious look all over her domain." Inside the church are painted texts of 17th century date and also memorials to the Sandys family of Graythwaite, who founded Hawkshead grammar school.

Methodist Chapel

The Methodist association is a charming little chapel, tucked away in one of the squares. In 1862, Mrs Satterthwaite, who was a member of the Society of Friends at Colthouse, purchased four cottages and "converted" one of them into a Free Church chapel, first known as Union Chapel, to be used by any Nonconformists who wished. After the death of its founder, it was handed over to the Methodist Church. Two stained glass windows on the west wall commemorate Mrs Satterthwaite and her daughter. The Garnett family provided a new communion table and rails.

Pilgrim's Way

Follow a path through the fields to Colthouse and visit the Friends Meeting House (key at a local farmhouse) and the Quaker burial ground at a junction of roads. From Colthouse, there are fair-weather views of Hawkshead in its context of rounded hills.

Stained glass in Hawkshead Chapel.

The Dalesman's Kirk

THE old-style dalesman was a plain man, with plain ways. His faith was strong and simple, uncluttered by too much theology. "If t'prayer books reet, it's reet; if not, chuck it on t'back of t'fire." An 18th century Rector of Ousby, as noted by Norman Nicholson in an anthology of the Lake District, was very much a man of the people.

Norman wrote: "It was his constant practice, after Sunday afternoon prayers, to accompany the leading men of his parish to the adjoining ale-house, when each man spent a penny, and only a penny; that done he set the younger men to play at football (of which he was a great promoter) and other rustical diversions."

The statesmen who, two centuries ago, occupied the family farms of the upper dales were once referred to as Nature's Quakers. It was sufficient for them to know that there was a God above and the Devil beneath, with a Day of Judgement lying ominously just beyond the horizon.

The old chapels of the dale country were squat, solid and unpretentious, as though the builders lacked the heart to compete with the magnificence of the fells. An exception was a Victorian church, such as St Mary's, Ambleside, where tower and spire reach up to almost 200 ft above the ground and tickle the passing clouds. Here the effect is pretentious – and the maintenance costs are high.

Dale chapels arose out of need rather than vanity. In a large parish, they spared the dalesfolk a long journey to the parish church. Or they met the needs of people habitually cut off from the main church by snow or flood. An old dales kirk crouches rather than stands on tiptoe. Look at it through half-closed eyes and it seems to resemble the rock outcrops round about.

In their plainness these chapels matched the spirit of the dalesfolk – those families who for generations had tended an unyielding landscape, among the rock outcrops and under a sky that weeped a hundred inches a year. Life was tolerable in summer but it could be heart-breaking in a winter that seemed to last half a year. There were periods in the deep midwinter when some farms did not have the sun's rays directly upon them.

The pre-Reformation term of "priest" was being widely used in Lakeland until recent times. There was an informality about worship. As the priest approached the kirk, a member of the congregation would ring the bell and all would tramp indoors for worship. One or two sheep dogs would seek out the warmest spot, near the stove, and wait patiently for the congregation to rise for the benediction, when they knew hometime had arrived.

At the pre-Reformation church of Cartmel Fell – a church dedicated to St Anthony, patron saint of charcoal-burners - the old faith lingered in images set in stained glass, as described by Mrs Humphry Ward in her novel *Helbeck of Bannisdale*. She wrote: "Above the moth-eaten table that replaced the ancient altar there still rose a window that breathed the very secrets of the old faith – a window of radiant fragments, piercing the twilight of the little church with strange uncomprehended things." Here stood "a golden St Anthony, a virginal St Margaret...In the very centre of the stone tracery, a woman lifted herself in bed to receive the Holy Oil – so pale, so eager still after all these centuries!"

It has been said of this secluded church that local people who were keen to save themselves a seven-mile walk to Cartmel Priory built it early in the 16th century. The old-time character of the place is sustained by 17th century woodwork, including box pews. There is a three-decker pulpit. Classically, the clerk used the bottom deck and the second deck was for the parson, who moved to the top deck for the sermon.

A Matter of "Whittlegate"

The dalesfolk expected t'priest to be "yan o' t'praying soart". Taking up additional employment was a necessity at a time when the cleric was entirely dependent upon the charity of his parishioners for his material well-being. The 18th century had dawned before any general attempt was made to provide for them independently of the "flock". The old custom of whittlegate permitted the priest to join a local family and have free board and lodging.

The curate in Newlands Vale was one of many who benefited from whittlegate. He moved from one farmhouse to another, like the modern tramp, having "no fixed abode. The curate at Coniston also enjoyed his whittlegate, for one day he might be lodging under the roof of a rough but homely farmer and on the next day would be the guest of Sir John le Fleming, the squire.

A good many parsons eked out their small stipend by undertaking additional work, such as that of schoolmaster, hence the ink stains and other active signs of school life adorning pews and tables. One of the last traces of the custom was at Stonethwaite, in Borrowdale where, as late as the year 1875, scholars gathered in the church for lessons.

Wonderful Walker

The most outstanding example of an industrious parson was Robert Walker (1709-1802), who became known as Wonderful Walker because of his varied skills. Walker was curate at Seathwaite, in his native Duddon Valley. He was the youngest and weakest of a large family. There was nowt for it but that he must be "bred a scholar".

Walker became a schoolteacher at Buttermere, married a lass who had a dowry of £40 ("the principal of which

Chair made by "Wonderful Walker."

91

was never touched") and eventually settled down as parson and schoolmaster at Seathwaite in 1736. This "wreckling" of the family died in 1802, aged 93.

He and his family developed the noble northern art of living off next to nowt. It was said of him that "his seat was within the rails of the altar, the communion table was his desk...and he employed himself at his spinning wheel, while the children were repeating their lessons by his side." Wordsworth, no mean hand at simple living, described Walker's busy life both in *The Excursion* and the Duddon Sonnets.

Wordsworth also related that Walker had but one luxury – a woollen covering to his family pew. The parson's own hands had spun the covering. His clerical activities were often carried out at night and he would spend his daytime hours teaching, gardening, attending to a few cows and sheep on the fellside, and much else. At Seathwaite there were no idle hands that the Devil might use!

The eight children of Robert Walker kept sharp eyes on the hedges as they walked along. Strands of wool cast by sheep were plucked from the ground or prickly bushes and taken home, to be carded, then spun. Evenings in their tiny cottage were spent in spinning wool while one of the family read aloud, usually from the Bible. Their clothing, "hodden grey", was of their own manufacture, as was their linen. If there was any surplus wool, Walker bore it on his back, over the fells, to sell it at the nearest market.

A man who met Walker in 1754 noted that he was "dressed in a coarse blue frock, trimmed with black horn buttons, a checked shirt...a coarse apron and a pair of great wooden-soled shoes plated with iron to preserve them." The parish register of Seathwaite chapel, recording his death in 1802, says "he was a man singular for his temperance, industry and integrity".

As curate, he had received £5 a year when he arrived and he never drew more than £50 during his long spell of service. He spent liberally only on the welfare of his 12 children. His (frugal) wife predeceased him by a few months. At his wife's funeral, although ninety years old and almost blind, he ordered that the bearers should be his own three daughters and a granddaughter. When he died, he was in his 67th year as curate of Seathwaite. Robert and his wife left £2,000 for the family to spend.

Cloggers and Brewers

Robert Southey recorded that the priest in Newlands valley spent part of his spare time making clogs, clothes and prints for butter. The Langdale curate of about 1789 supplemented his income by opening a tavern and brewing the ale he served in it.

Mrs Mattinson, whose husband was curate of Patterdale from 1715 to 1763, charged a shilling for each birth she attended, plus "culinary perquisities". These last included cooking the food eaten at christening parties, payment for which prompted her to wish the mothers a speedy recovery and an "early return of such blessings."

Southey, entering the churchyard at Wasdale Head in 1802, was surprised to find well-designed and well-lettered tombstones of good red stone "in a place apparently inhabited by none but poor peasantry." The income of the Wasdale parson was about £20 a year, most of it coming from Queen Anne's bounty.

In 1845, Wasdale Head church had "neither enclosing fence nor doors, a thorn bush seeming to keep out sheep. The church was bedded with bracken like a stable; there were two pews and the other seats were sheep forms on trestles." Provost Fox referred to "a congregation of smells, like Wasdale Head chapel in sheep-shearing time."

The Lakeland clerics were, almost to a man, characters – men with distinctive personalities. Old Sewell, of Wythburn, by Thirlmere, was a shepherd in duplicate, having care of many souls and the ownership of a lusty flock of herdwick sheep. While preaching in his run-down church, his sermon notes vanished into a crack beside the pulpit. He was not unduly upset and offered to read "a chapter o' the Bible worth ten of it."

Wythburn was referred to by Wordsworth, in *The Waggoner*, as a "modest house of prayer...As lowly as the lowliest dwelling." The church had a single bell to summon the godly to church. When the bell-ringer was found sitting astride the roof ridge, and ringing the bell by hand, he told inquirers that Jemmy Hawkrigg had borrowed the rope for his hay cart.

Parson Lawson (1849-1852) needed to diversify his work. Payment of his modest salary should have taken place in half-yearly instalments. In November, 1850, he noted on two successive days that it was due. A week later, he wrote: "Went to Keswick. Received salary."

Poor Swindale

A writer in the *Pall Mall Gazette* in 1894 stated of Swindale chapel that it is "a poor wan little church: damp, thanks to the south-west wind and its rain, and also to the clustering sycamores which do their best to hide it. Ten pews or so, each adapted for about four persons of ordinary breadth, make up its complement. It has no lavish decoration; indeed no decoration at all, except three or four faded coarse little symbolic frescoes on its pallid walls and a meagre beading to the colour wash by the windows."

W G Collingwood, in a note about Swindale in the 19th century, wrote: "One clergyman, when the parsonage had become too ruinous, lived from house to house, and carried his box of sermons with him. He took one out of the top, when Sunday came, without much picking and choosing, until the old lady with whom he lodged told me to "stir up that box'; they're beginning to come varra thick", as if they were porridge.

The church had an iron stove, "the plainest of plain stone font and a naked altar. These, with the hempen bellrope, constitute its movables. The love that the congregation bear to such a building must be of the profound, the heartfelt kind. There is not an aesthetic touch about the church."

Consider Richard Birkett, the parson at Martindale for 67 years. When he arrived in this remote valley near Ullswater, he had two shirts and a suit of clothes. He drew less than £3 a year from the church and had to take on other jobs. He married a woman who had £60. When Birkett died, she could put her hands on £1,200.

In Birkett's time, Easter dues were paid in eggs. The farmers were soon made to realise that they could not dispose of small eggs by giving them to the parson, for he used a special gauge - a board in which a hole had been cut. If an egg passed through the hole, it was handed back to the farmer who had brought it.

John Stuart Mill (1831) found the roof of Grasmere church consisting of naked slates, whitewashed internally, with all the junctures visible and lots of old bare rafters. "There are only one or two pews, and those of the simplest and most unpretending kind. Every thing however that admitted of it was hung with bouquets and festoons of fresh flowers, intermixed with some quaint bunches of feathers; the rustic character of the ornaments harmonised as much as their gaudy colours contrasted with the homely appearance of the building."

Wedding Days

Owd Sarah Yewdale, who was called Queen of Borrowdale, recalled when folk went to church on horseback. On wedding days, nearly everyone and every horse was be-ribboned, though "some stole off as they do now to be wedded, and never a dog barked. Nobody was wiser until it was all over."

Folk generally made "a great do" of weddings. "There'd be as many as 20 or 30 go to the kirk on nag's back...It was a very cheerful sight to see them all going down the road in a long string on a fine morning." Owd Sarah added: "There were sad sights coming back, such galloping and clattering, and you might have thought all Borrowdale was gone mad, for you see it was reckoned a great thing to be first home from the kirk. There was Jack Bennett – Gentleman Jack, as we called him – who had a mare called Kate that no one could beat. Many's the time that Kate has come home first, and not always with anybody on her back."

After dinner was over, folk came in from all parts of the dale. "The bride sat in the porch with a wood dish on her knees, and everybody gave her summat, presenting it cheerfully, and she wasn't ashamed to take it...But folk got ower proud to be beholden to one another and 'bidden weddings' went out of fashion."

Among the best-known legends relating to the 18th century is that of the Bishop of Barf. A mile or two from Keswick, along the Bassenthwaite road to Cockermouth, is the Swan Hotel, once known as the Swan with Two Necks. High on Barf, and just above a loose scree, is a white rock that is visible from afar. A bishop staying at the Swan in about 1793 wagered he could not only reach the pulpit-shaped rock on Barf but he could do so on horseback. The deed was done but after passing the rock, the horse stumbled, fell and died. A second white-painted rock marking the horse's grave was referred to as The Clerk.

The Rushbearing

Years ago, the earthen floors of many country churches were strewn with fresh rushes. Each summer, the old covering was removed and fresh rushes strewn. It became a time of celebration that was formalised in 1812 when St Annes, the hillside church at Ambleside, was re-built and flagged. The Rev Owen Lloyd, who was the curate in the year 1835, composed the Rushbearers' Hymn.

Lloyd was originally a Quaker, son of Charles Lloyd of Brathay. He was baptised as an adult, confirmed and ordained in the Church of England. He based his hymn on Isaiah 35, verses 1, 2 and 7, and it was sung to the tune *Irish*. The words were not profound but suited the occasion:

> Our fathers to the House of God,
>   As yet a building rude,
> Bore offerings from the flowery sod,
>   And fragrant rushes strew'd.

> May we, their children, ne'er forget
>   The pious lesson given,
> But honour still, together met,
>   The Lord of Earth and Heaven!

> Sing we the good Creator's praise,
>   Who sends us sun and showers,
> To cheer our hearts with fruitful days,
>   And deck our world with flowers!

> These, of the great Redeemer's grace,
>   Bright emblems here are seen!
> He makes to smile the desert place
>   With flowers and rushes green.

The Rushbearing was linked with St Anne's Day, July 26, and when first planned it took place on the nearest Saturday. This date, falling in the school holidays, was not convenient for many and so the ceremony was moved to the Saturday nearest July 2. At the Rush-bearing, reeds and rushes gathered from the lakes and tarns are woven with flowers on to wooden frames of various designs, being referred to as "bearings".

On the great day, a procession begins at the school near St Mary's and tours the town to the market place, where the special hymn is sung. The bearings are lifted high for a moment to ensure that everyone in the assembled crowd can see them. The procession is resumed. A service is held in church and the bearings are left there, while all who have carried them receive some gingerbread.

During the 1939-45 war, a student at the Royal College of Art, which had been evacuated to Ambleside, painted a mural - 26ft long, 12ft high – in St Mary's. The work, carried out in powder colours, with an oil size emulsion, was completed in four months.

Pilgrimage 18 – The Heart of Wordsworthshire

Grasmere, possibly the most famous village in the Lake District, is beside the main road, A591, to the north of Ambleside. William Wordsworth resided in Grasmere when he wrote some of his finest verse and, as Norman Nicholson, a modern poet, wrote, covered the fells and dales in "the comfortable warmth of religiosity." Go to Grasmere – and simply follow the signs!

The Wordsworths

William and Dorothy, his sister, set up house at Dove Cottage, Grasmere, on a crisp December day in 1799. They had travelled from Kendal by post-chaise and, on their journey northwards, doubtless watched the interplay of light on snow-covered hills. It was almost dark when the chaise lurched its way along a rough road into the Vale of Grasmere. At five o'clock they were put down outside Dove Cottage.

Molly Fisher, who was to be their daily help, greeted them in a stone-flagged room in which a fire was ablaze. William (1770-1850), who became one of England's premier poets, was a Cumbrian, born at Cockermouth. He and his sister became friends of Samuel Taylor Coleridge and his brother-in-law, Robert Southey, and in due course all settled in the Lake District.

In 1802, Wordsworth married a childhood acquaintance, Mary Hutchinson. The Wordsworths (including sister Dorothy) moved from Dove Cottage to Allan Bank, then (with a growing family) to the Parsonage and finally to Rydal Hall, in the next village.

A Churchman

William, who in his young days had been a revolutionary, became one of the Establishment, regularly occupying the family pew in Grasmere and later Rydal churches and taking an interest in plans for the big new church at Ambleside, which would be dedicated to St Mary.

Wordsworth saw and approved the plans but died before work on the site began. The church stands on solid rock – so solid, indeed, that when a new vestry was made in 1968 workmen tackled a great lump of rock with pneumatic drills. The tower holds a clock. It has no outward faces, yet the chiming of the bells punctuates the Ambleside day.

The Wordsworth chapel is an attraction for many. Friends and admirers of the poet's work living in this country and America subscribed towards the cost of a window to his memory. In 1952, during celebrations to mark the centenary of the poet's death, this part of the church was furnished as a chapel. In it are two chairs that once stood in the poet's home at Rydal Mount. The widow of Wordsworth, who attended the dedication of St Mary's in 1854, gave the Bible for the lectern. Other members of the Wordsworth family have their memorial windows.

High Victorian

A Lakeland pilgrim will assuredly stop at St Mary's, which has all the stolid self assurance of the Victorian age – an age that had its local flowering following the coming of the railway to Windermere. When it was considered necessary to replace St Anne's, the church on a steep hillside, a green-field site was adopted and the chosen architect was Gilbert Scott.

A century passed. The great weight of the spire was pressing down on the walls to such ill effect that cracks appeared in the masonry of the tower. What should be done? A majority of parishioners requested the removal of the spire, partly on aesthetic grounds, yet when a public meeting was called almost all of those present voted in favour of strengthening the tower so that it could continue to carry the spire. The work, completed just before the centenary celebrations, cost over £7,000.

As it had been Wordsworth's influence that led to Mr Benson Harrison donating a large sum to the building fund, and as the Poet himself had also contributed, it was decided to honour him by placing a memorial window in the church.

Grasmere Church

This is a successor to one which (according to legend) was set up shortly after St Oswald had preached here in the 7th century. Wordsworth, a regular church-goer, describes St Oswald's Church in Book V of *The Excursion:*

Not raised in nice proportion was the pile;
But large and massy; for duration built;
With pillars crowded, and the roof upheld
By naked rafters intricately crossed,
Like leafless underboughs in some thick wood...
   The floor
Of nave and aisle, in unprentending guise,
Was occupied by oaken benches ranged
In seemly rows...An heraldic shield,
Varying its tincture with the changeful light,
Imbued the altar-window; fixed aloft
A faded hatchment hung, and one by time
Yet undiscoloured. A capacious pew
Of sculptured oak stood here, with drapery lined.

The building is massive, heavily rendered, not picturesque outside but decided-ly quaint inside, where a row of shallow arches rests on square pillars. Thus was the church enlarged by adding a new aisle to the north, then cutting holes in the original north wall to leave "pillars". The "thick wood" of "intricately crossed" rafters was needed to raise the roof after the north aisle had been added. No longer are there oaken benches; they have been replaced by pews.

In later life, Wordsworth attended a church at Rydal that had been built in his lifetime by Lady le Fleming in what had been an orchard. In 1830, John Ruskin (aged 11) was on a tour of the Lake District with his parents when they attended this place of worship.

Young Ruskin wrote in his diary: "We were lucky in procuring a seat very near that of Mr Wordsworth, there being only one between it and the one we were in. We were rather disappointed in this gentleman's appearance especially as he appeared asleep the greatest part of the time. He seemed about 60. This gentleman possesses a long face and a large nose with a moderate assortment of grey hairs and 2 small eyes grey not filled with fury wrapt inspired with a mouth of moderate dimensions that is quite large enough to let in a sufficient quantity of beef or mutton & to let out a sufficient quantity of poetry."

Pilgrim's Way

When visiting Grasmere, park your car at White Moss Common (NG 348066), courtesy of the National Trust, who have set up display panels showing walking routes. The path to be chosen dips to a bridge near the outflow of Grasmere, a lake that is a mile long and rather more than half a mile wide. In good weather, there is an enchanting view of the lake, the fells and woodland holding a thousand shades of green. Also in view is the dun-coloured Prince of Wales Hotel.

The main path leads to the road, beside which Victorian mansions stand behind screens of beech hedges, mossy walls and "private" notices. An exception is Wyke Cottage, named after a local gill – or ghyll, as Wordsworth was fond of writing – and as pretty as a picture on the lid of a chocolate-box. Wordsworth, who knew the cottage and wrote a poem based on the resident Mackereth family, would not have described it so.

The island on the lake, complete with restored barn, has changed from Wordsworth's "solitary green island" to one with many lusty trees and shrubs. Old folk relate when sheep had their legs tied and were placed in a low, flat-bottomed boat that was hauled by rowing boat to and from the island grazings. Pass the suburbs of Grasmere and the boat landing, from which visitors row to or around the island.

After visiting Grasmere Church, walk on to see Dove Cottage. The Prince of Wales Hotel and some soundly-built Victorian buildings have long blocked the view that the Wordsworths had from Dove Cottage (a property that William and Dorothy knew as Town End, after the hamlet in which it stood). The building is now garlanded by roses and looks more attractive than it must have done when the Wordsworths were here. The Dove Cottage Trust owns the property and much else in Town End. They have opened a splendid museum and scholars from all over the world consult tomes in a fine library housed in another building.

Follow the high road to White Moss, where the pilgrimage circuit is completed. Before leaving, ponder on the Wordsworths of Dove Cottage, which incidentally had been an inn. They watched with sustained interest the passing traffic – beggers, peddlers, waggoners and, eventually, tourists – using the route over White Moss Common. William Wordsworth bestowed immortality on some of the passers-by, such as Benjamin the waggoner, by mentioning them in verse.

Pilgrimage 19 – Rawnsley of Crosthwaite

Crosthwaite Church stands in a quiet cul de sac to the north of Keswick.

Basic Details

The spirit of Canon Hardwicke Rawnsley still broods over Crosthwaite Church. He was a powerful preacher, an incessant writer of sermons, poems and books about the Lake District, and one of the founders of the National Trust – a man worthy of pilgrimage.

In 1883, Bishop Goodwin of Carlisle offered Rawnsley the living of Crosthwaite. Wrote the Bishop: "The vicarage, as you know, is simply charming...In my opinion, the post which I offer you is as near heaven as anything in this world can be." Rawnsley was inducted on July 8, 1883 and virtually his first act was to toll the bell 64 times and, after a pause, a further 41.

At Crosthwaite vicarage, he lost no time in carving in the stone on top of the terrace wall some words of Thomas Gray, an early tourist in the Lake District. Gray (1789) had written: "I got to the parsonage a little before sunset and saw in my [Claude] glass a picture that, if I could transmit to you, and fix in it all the softness of its living colours, would fairly sell for a thousand pounds. This is the sweetest scene I can yet discover in point of pastoral beauty." The cedar tree in Crosthwaite churchyard may have grown from the cone that Rawnsley brought back from a visit to Lebanon.

Canon Rawnsley enlivened his parish magazine with incidents of national importance. Other topics he broached were re-housing, pure milk supply and the prevention of tuberculosis. He became a Canon of Carlisle Cathedral and joined in the varied activities of Keswick, to the extent of sitting on committees.

Rawnsley established the Lake District Defence Society, which was to be superseded by the Friends of the Lake District. After the foundation of the National

Trust in 1895, he saw to it that many properties in the Lake District were acquired.

Rawnsley's photograph might be seen, on request, in the vestry of Crosthwaite Church. Rawnsley, a great activist, designed the gate to the churchyard, which features various Celtic motifs, including a salmon and a bell.

Pilgrim's Way

See Pilgrimage No. 6, which also leads to Crosthwaite Church. Or walk from the centre of Grasmere along the road which passes near Allan Banks, where Rawnsley died and from which his widow, Edith, organised festivals of local interest. The walk offers enchanting views of Grasmere and its flanking fells.

Pilgrimage 20 – The Lost Church of Mardale

Mardale ceased to exist when Manchester Corporation built a reservoir. Today, Haweswater laps and frets against a backdrop of shapely fells. Approach the area from Shap via Bampton (the approach is well-marked). The road beside Haweswater is a cul de sac, ending at a usually crowded car park. Instead, leave the car at a suitable place in Burnbanks, the village created by Manchester, and walk along the quiet western shore of the reservoir.

Basic Details

Mardale Church, dedicated to the Holy Trinity, was one of the smallest in Lakeland, being comparable with Wasdale Head, Wythburn and Swindale. It had seating for 50 people and, towards the end of its life, served a total population of about 70. Worshippers were summoned by the clanging of a bell that had been cast in 1825.

The first reference to Mardale, in 1670, is taken to prove the existence of a church at that time. At the Dissolution of the Monasteries, Mardale became part of the extensive Shap parish. The last building to serve the district was of 17th century date, having walls 3 ft thick. A special feature was the oaken gallery, dated 1737. It was installed when an oak screen and communion rails were fitted.

Interments

The first burial, of John Turner, who had lived at Mardale Green, took place in 1729. Prior to this a dead person was conveyed, strapped to the back of a horse or pony, up the zig-zags of what became known as the Corpse Road, which crests at 1,656 ft and leads to Swindale and Shap.

Shap Abbey.

Hall Caine, in his novel *The Shadow of a Crime*, told how some wicked man died in Mardale with an undivulged crime on his conscience. As his coffin, strapped to the back of a horse, was in transit to Shap for burial, a thunderstorm arose and the horse bolted. For three months it roamed Swindale Common, an area with many humps and hollows. The coffin remained on its back. In due course, the horse was re-captured. The man was buried at Shap.

Mardale was granted its own burial ground when local people complained of the distance to the parish church causing "excessive expense for funerals" and declaring that "the souls as well as the bodies of infants taken to be baptised are endangered." When, in 1898, seven-year-old Isaac Edmondson, of Flake How, died, the verse selected by the Vicar reflected the staunch religious faith of that period:

Sleep on, beloved! Sleep and take thy rest,
Lay down thy head upon thy Saviour's breast;
We loved thee well, but Jesus loves thee best.
Good-night.

Parish Life

One vicar was the energetic Rev W Terry, who was here for 16 years. The Rev J Whiteside, Vicar of Shap, wrote of the Rev Terry that "he remains a model to the fellside clergy whose lot is cast in very lonely and difficult surroundings." He introduced slide shows on topics as diverse as "Paying Poultry" and "Mission Work in Japan". The phonograph brought tinny recorded music into the dale.

The reservoir-work began when engineers made trial holes in 1929. The work closed down due to recession in 1931 and opened up again in 1934. Haweswater's immense dam was completed in 1941 and that same year water was creaming over the spillway.

Pilgrim's Way

Follow the footpath from Burnbanks along the shore of Haweswater. The old settlement of Mardale stood round about the area where Riggindale gives way to the main valley. Then visit the cemetery just beyond Shap Church and look at tombstones and graves of Mardale folk who, when the reservoir was being built, were re-interred here.

Indomitable Women

Pilgrimage 21 – Lady Anne Clifford (1590-1676)

The Lady Anne Trail, devised in 1990 by Eden Tourism Action Programme, in collaboration with English Heritage and with the support of District Councils and Tourist Boards, invited the reader to "follow in the footsteps of this indomitable woman" just four centuries after her birth. Information about the Trail is available from Tourist Information Centres between Skipton and Penrith.

Lady Anne Clifford.

ANNE CLIFFORD was almost a queen on her family estates. One of her many biographers, C M Bouch, pictured her holding her court in her various castles; moving in her coach-and-four from one to the other on the appointed days, attended by a great retinue of servants and officials, "yet in her own person and life giving an example of simplicity and frugality."

She was also pious. During the Commonwealth, when people were forbidden to use the Liturgy of the Anglican Church, she refused to Communicate in any other way. Each of her houses had a chaplain and every morning she heard prayers and a chapter from the Bible.

Lady Anne, the last of the illustrous Cliffords of Skipton and Westmorland, had five castles – Skipton, Pendragon, Brough, Appleby and Brougham. Her favourite, Brougham, was where her father had been born and her mother died. She worshipped in a tiny chapel near the top of the keep and attended services at several churches she had restored, and especially at Ninekirks, now in the middle of a field. It stands unaltered since her day. Mr Grasty, who was incumbent at Ninekirks for 12 years, was familiar with her tiny figure, clad in rough black serge, "a dress not disliked by any yet imitated by none".

Lady Anne was born on January 30, 1590, being the only daughter of George, 13th Lord Clifford and 3rd Earl of Cumberland, and Margaret, a daughter of the Earl of Bedford. As a youngster, Lady Anne experienced the splendour of Queen Elizabeth's court, at which her father was Queen's champion. Anne married twice – first, at the age of 19, to Richard Sackville, Lord Bathurst, who shortly succeeded to the title of Earl of Dorset. They had five children, of which two survived infancy.

Smallpox, endemic in those days, was the scourge of both rich and poor. When her daughter Margaret was 10, she contracted smallpox. Lady Anne nursed her and was in turn a victim of a disfiguring disease which badly marked them both. The blemishes were diplomatically ignored by the artists commissioned to paint portraits of her Ladyship.

After 15 years of marriage, her husband died. Seven years later, she married Philip Herbert, 4th Earl of Pembroke and Montgomery. He was a wild character but, being a Parliamentarian at the right time, gave his wife, a Royalist, a chance to inherit her northern estates, which were at risk in the troublesome days of the Civil War.

There were long years of controversy, of wrangling and of lawsuits relating to her claim to the Clifford lands. Eventually, and by now widowed for a second time, she had her determination to take over the Clifford lands rewarded. Lady Anne joyfully regained her rights and returned to the North in 1649. The rest of her life was spent in restoring and managing her big estates.

Lady Anne's full title was impressive – Countess Dowager of Dorset, Pembroke and Montgomery, Baroness Clifford, Westmorland and Vesey, Lady of the Honour of Skipton-in-Craven and Hereditary Sheriffess of Westmorland. Yet she had the happy knack of making an appeal to people in all walks of life – from bishops to the little old ladies who occupied her almshouses. She was fond of presenting gifts to friends and visitors, noting each in her great diary.

The favourite portraits of her were copied for distribution among family and close friends. She even distributed locks and keys made for her at Appleby by George Dent, who charged her £1 each. Among the recipients were the Hasells of Dalemain, near Ullswater, and Bishop Rainbow of Rose Castle. They were dutifully put into use. Presumably, Lady Anne had a spare key.

Cheerfully ignoring Cromwell, she rebuilt her castles, thus maintaining a medieval way of life when a new age had dawned. In 1651, masons, joiners and lead-beaters worked on Caesar's Tower at her castle in Appleby. New floors and rooms were constructed. The roof was raised 80 feet and covered with lead. From the tower, she had a panoramic view of the Pennines, including the great notch of High Cup Nick.

Boroughgate at Appleby was transformed when work on the castle was put in hand and new almshouses were built for the accommodation of a "mother, reader and twelve sisters". In the church, her vault was excavated during her lifetime. She would repose beside the splendidly adorned tomb of her mother.

With five castles, she travelled a good deal during the drier time of the year. Her litter was slung between two horses in tandem while her attendant ladies rode in a coach drawn by six horses. Holding the reins was Edward Smith, her devoted coachman. Friends, more servants and guards followed the coach on horseback.

The sight of Lady Anne's cavalcade brought a splash of colour to dun-coloured uplands. She loved to use unusual routes, such as the Stake Pass between Wharfedale and Wensleydale, and over Cotter Riggs and along Abbotside Common to Hell Gill, where a packhorse bridge crossed the narrow gorge of the infant Eden.

When going over Cotter Riggs, she was en route from Nappa Hall, a kinsman's house in Wensleydale, to her castle of Pendragon, which was set in the midst of Mallerstang Forest. Pendragon had been put into a habitable state and Mr Branthwaite, who resided here, received a special allowance towards the cost of keeping the coal fires burning, the fuel being mined at small pits on Tan Hill.

Innumerable inscriptions ensured that her generosity was not forgotten. The Countess Pillar, which she caused to be raised by the main road at Brougham, commemorated the place where she had her last parting from her mother. Anne's second marriage had not been happy and at a time when she and her husband were estranged, she travelled North to stay with her mother. The parting came when she decided to return to her husband.

The date for the departure was April 2, 1616. Her mother accompanied her as far as the park gate. Soon after Anne had returned home, she received the news that her mother had died. Mother had stood by her in her adversity while suffering from the unfaithfulness of her husband, George Clifford, who on his death-bed sent her a letter asking forgiveness for all the wrongs he had done her.

Typically, on having the commemorative pillar raised, the dutiful daughter, Lady Anne, "left an annuity of four pounds to be distributed to ye poor within this Parish of Brougham every 2nd day of April for ever upon ye stone table here hard by." Her wish is still carried out.

Lady Anne died on March 22, 1676, aged 86 years. She passed away in her own room, above the inner gateway, after four days of pain and sickness. She had probably suffered a heart attack. Her last recorded words were: "I thank God I am very well."

Lady Anne's tomb at St Lawrence's, Appleby, awaited her ancient body. The tomb was emblazoned by heraldry depicting the marriages of her Clifford fore-bears. A lead-shell coffin, no more than 4 ft 10 in long, was borne down eight steps into a vault 6 ft high, 9 ft square. Edward Rainbow, Bishop of Carlisle, preached for three hours using the text: "Every wise woman buildeth her house."

Pilgrim's Way

Go to Appleby, park the car near the swimming pool and walk by the river, thence up Boroughgate, one of the finest streets in England, sloping with grace-ful properties on either side, having a castle at the top and the parish church at the bottom. The High Cross carries an inscription which mirrors the life of Lady Anne – "Retain your loyalty,/ Preserve your right."

On the way up Boroughgate, call at the almshouses (left, near the top). Lady Anne founded the hospital, as it was then known, for the aged women of Appleby and she was present when the foundation stone was laid in April, 1651. The foun-dation provides rooms for a Mother and twelve Sisters. The visitor passes under an archway into a cobbled yard, flanked by the redstone homes and with a chapel in one corner that is opened up on request. Inside is a studded and dated chest given by Lady Anne.

Now visit the Castle and, if it is "open to view", enter the Great Hall to take a close look at a tryptych painting relating to Lady Anne. Climb the keep by a spiral staircase and look out over the town and the dale to the Pennines. On the way back to the car, call at St Lawrence's Church to look at the tombs of Lady Anne and her mother (in the corner, left of the altar).

Escape again from the hub-hub of the modern world by parking the car beside the A66 to the east of Penrith. Look out for the Countess Pillar, which has been re-sited on higher ground where a cutting was made for an improved highway. Further, on the left, is a small parking area, fenced round, which is the starting point for a short walk near the Eamont and on to the field where the church of St Wilfred of Brougham, commonly called Ninekirks, stands (GR 559299). This walk is more fully described on page 39.

Lady Anne caused the old structure "to be new built up again at the same place larger and bigger than it was before" adding that it "would in all likelyhood have fallen down, it was so ruinous, if it had not bin repaired by me." The church is almost as she left it, with a font dated 1662, an almsbox carved with the words "Remember the Poor", dated 1663, and pews in panelled enclosures.

Pilgrimage 22 – Harriet Martineau (1802-1876)

Harriet Martineau, a radical who became the first English woman journalist of note, built herself a house at Ambleside and called it The Knoll. It is not "open to view" but if you visit the new Armitt Library, in premises just inside the gates of Charlotte Mason College, you will find a section is devoted to Harriet and her Lakeland associations.

Harriet's bright spirit enabled her to overcome ill health, including deafness, and to leave for our delectation books, articles and pamphlets revealing a lively mind and thoughts that were usually about 20 years ahead of her time. At the age of 21, she wrote a theological novel followed – between 1832 and 1834 – by a nine-volume work on political economy. She talked. She travelled. She wrote over 1,600 leading articles for the *Daily News* and contributed to influential magazines.

Her interests ranged from the improvement of agricultural crops (against a background of the potato famine in Ireland), sanitation and building societies. She was born in Norfolk in 1802, being the daughter of a wealthy manufacturer of French descent. Harriet Martineau described her unhappy childhood as her winter. The years of literary recognition formed her stormy spring – and the long summer of her life was the period when she lived in Ambleside, an area she had known from holidays spent at Windermere.

Harriet moved into her new home with two servants, oddments of furniture donated by friends, books and files. She managed to communicate despite grave physical disabilities, especially of hearing. She had been a sickly child and bouts of ill-health were to recur throughout her life. Harriet, a native of Norwich, was not overtly a religious person after her break with Unitarianism. Throughout her life she sought a type of spirituality that would suit her and came close to her dream at Ambleside, close to the mountains, where she had clean air and the stimulus of conversations with cultured people.

Among her new friends were the Wordsworths, who lived a short distance up the road at Ryda, though it would have been interesting to overhear a conversation in which Harriet used an ear-trumpet and Wordsworth tried to communicate without the help of his teeth.

Matthew Arnold, who had a house Under Loughrigg, was among those dismayed at Harriet's rejection of orthodox Christian beliefs, such as the notion of a personal God. He told a friend he had "talked to Miss Martineau – who blasphemes frightfully." Caring for the oppressed was part of her philosophy. She was particularly conscious, following a visit to North America, of the plight of black American slaves.

This too-long-forgotten lady of letters moved on impulse to Ambleside in 1846. The view from The Knoll took in meadowland to the River Rothay and up to Loughrigg. Harriet was so thrilled by the pastoral vista she felt that if she blinked it might melt. Her love of Lakeland expressed itself in her *Guide to the English Lakes* (1855), published at a time when the coming of the railway to Windermere had created a building boom and many changes in local life.

She wrote well and could be bitingly critical, such as when the huge St Mary's Church was built in what had been a green and pleasant landscape within sight of her home. She described the church as "more of a blemish than an adornment, unhappily, from its size and clumsiness and the bad taste of its architecture. Though placed in a valley, it has a spire – the appropriate form of churches in a level country...and the east window is remarkably ugly."

When I re-published Harriet's *A Guide to Windermere*, which had first appeared under the imprint of John Garnett of Windermere in 1854, a foreword was provided by Nigel Holmes, of BBC Radio Cumbria, who quoted a contemporary comment that Harriet "is the most continual talker I ever heard. It is really like the babbling of a brook and very lively and sensible, too." Harriet used her ear-trumpet like a microphone, directing it towards the people in the room, yet she was clearly a popular and effective speaker. The partition wall in the Methodist chapel had to be removed to accommodate all who came to hear her lecture, whether on domestic topics or her distant travels.

For a century after her death in 1876, Harriet Martineau, this interesting, controversial character, was almost forgotten. Today, she has her friends who are giving her literary reputation a kiss of life. Harriet had known many famous people, such as Charlotte Bronte and her biographer, Mrs Gaskell, Charles Dickens and George Eliot. She corrresponded with them and they stayed with her. She said what she thought and Charlotte Bronte, who was here in 1850, retired hurt after criticism of *Villette*.

Charlotte had written to her friend Ellen Nussey: "Her house is very pleasant, both within and without; arranged at all points with admirable neatness and comfort. Her visitors enjoy the most perfect liberty; what she claims for herself she allows them. I rise at my own hour, breakfast alone (she is up at five, takes a cold bath, and a walk by starlight, and has finished breakfast and got to her work by seven o' clock)."

Despite her sharp manner and words, many of her Lakeland contemporaries seem to have been fond of her eccentricities. When the weekly wash was completed on Monday, the soap suds were used to bathe the pig she kept at a small farm near her home. She felt the pig was much happier for being clean and, as a result, yielded better bacon. Harriet was acutely aware of hygene; she washed everything in sight and had a flush toilet. She cared for her servants, teaching some of them geography and offering the use of her home for a wedding reception for a servant who was to be married.

We can still enjoy much of her prose, especially her Lakeland guide. One example is her commendation of Ferry Nab, on the southern side of Bowness Bay. To her it was a charming resting-place. "It is breezy here; and the waters smack the shore cheerily."

Pilgrim's Way

Park the car in the big park not far from the House on the Bridge. Cross the road to visit the Armitt Library, with its section on Harriet Martineau. Then re-cross the road and take a path through Rothay Park, having a glimpse of The Knoll, which is now divided into two dwellings. After crossing the Rothay by bridge, turn left, then – at the first opportunity – left again and stroll slowly back through this fascinating Victorian town, noticing Fairfield, the local mountain where, Harriet noted, "an old shepherd had charge of four rain gauges, set up on four ridges – desolate, misty spots, sometimes below and often above the clouds."

Pilgrimage 23 – Princess at Finsthwaite

A pilgrimage with a difference, taking in a wooded hill with a tower of naval interest, a dam that has similarities with a Scottish lochan – and the grave reputed to have connections with Bonnie Prince Charlie. Finsthwaite is tucked away near Lakeside, where Windermere overflows as the River Leven.

The story of the mysterious lady who has lain buried in Finsthwaite churchyard since 1771 in the name of Clementina Johannes Sobiesky Douglass, of Waterside, is fascinating. Was she a Polish princess? Or a daughter of Prince Charles Edward Stuart by his mistress Clementina Walkenshaw? Or yet again the God-daughter of his mother, Clementina Sobiesky? No one knows for sure.

The conclusion that she was an illegitimate daughter of Bonnie Prince Charlie is almost irresistible. Who was James Douglass, the man who was said to have brought the so-called princess to this secluded Lakeland village? Could she, in 1745, have accompanied the army of the Bonnie Prince on his disastrous march to Derby, being left at Kendal, which was a safe retreat from those who disliked the Stuarts?

Theories abound. H E Barker, who lived at Haverthwaite, thought she might well have been a delicate and perhaps weak-minded girl whose behaviour embarrassed her parents. Business and family connections between people in this part of Furness and those in the West of Scotland being strong, perhaps she was brought to Finsthwaite to be cared for by a Mr and Mrs Backhouse.

Was she therefore no more than someone of humble status who was spoken of locally as "princess" because she put on airs? Mr Barker remembered a "Countess" who was really a domestic servant. "Who then would deny an 18th century village 'princess', especially when we in these days have so many pretty girls exalted to the ranks of beauty queens?...I would be inclined...to forget about Jacobites and Jacobins; the Old Pretender and the Young Pretender...and instead concentrate on the activities of the early industrial adventurers whose interests were divided between Scotland and this part of Furness."

In 1913, the grave of the mysterious Finsthwaite Princess, having become effaced, and known only to a few of the older folk in the village, a stone was erected to perpetuate her memory.

Pilgrim's Way

Faced with a choice of starting points for Finsthwaite, and in the mood to take your time before visiting Finsthwaite churchyard, park your car in a roadside space near the Newby Bridge halt on the Haverthwaite-Lakeside Railway. Just across the road is the Leven, with an attendant dipper – a podgy little bird with a white "bib", which may do no more than watch you as it "courtseys" on a water-washed stone.

Walk towards the Swan Hotel, then turned left to cross the railway, and left again. A sign (right) indicates the path to Finsthwaite Tower – a path that is at first constricted, with a flight of stone steps, before leading you a deciduous wood where the trees are mainly oak. You will climb steadily, with more stone steps and an easy scramble over outcropping rock to a grassy knoll – a viewpoint for Gummers How, a hill beyond gleaming Windermere lake.

Return a few paces to a path going off left to Finsthwaite Tower, built at a viewpoint that is now flanked by mature trees and, in its ruined state, like an old temple in a jungle. Here are commemorated Admiral Nelson and his admirals who waged war against the Fleets of France and Spain. The path from the Tower dips into a dell and eventually reaches a stile in a wood.

You will see, two fields ahead, the spired outline of Finsthwaite church. A marble cross, commemorating the Finsthwaite Princess, is quite near the back of the building. Extend your pilgrimage, if there is time and the day is bright, to visit

High Dam via Plum Green. You may rest beside a stretch of water on which there is an island adorned, Scottish fashion, with pine and ling.

There remains the pleasant task of walking back to Tilberthwaite and to a point near Finsthwaite House where a bridleway begins, having a pleasant woodland course before descending to the railway beside which you left your car.

On the High Hills

Pilgrimage 24 – Great Gable

A sacred place? Having a war memorial on its rocky crest sanctifies Gable.
This records the names of members of the Fell and Rock Climbing Club who
gave their lives. The Club gave the fell and others to the National Trust. Many
walkers leave their cars by Honister Pass, at 1,176 ft, crossing the tops of
Grey Knotts, Brandreth and Green Gable. The recommended pilgrim's route
is a climb of 2,700 unremitting feet from Seathwaite, in Borrowdale (GR
235122), which is reached from Keswick, travelling southwards through
Borrowdale.

THIS PILGRIMAGE IS FOR THOSE FAMILIAR WITH FELL-WALKING
WHO HAVE COMPASS, MAP AND WATERPROOF GARB IN CASE THE
WEATHER TURNS NASTY.

Basic Details

Gable, viewed from Wasdale, is triangular – everyone's idea of a mountain. It takes central position on the emblem of the Lake District National Park. With a height of 2,949 ft, Gable seems to block out half the sky. The upper reaches form a rockscape, and much of the rock is loose and clinks underfoot. The crags have attracted climbers since Victorian days, when W P Haskett-Smith climbed Napes Needle, our most famous rock stack, repeating the feat half a century later, at the age of 74. It is not recommended for pilgrims.

Pilgrim's Way

The object is to reach the summit by 11 a.m., on the 11th day of the 11th month, which is the time and day on which the guns fell silent after the Great War. On my last visit, with David Johnstone and his lively collie, Popsie, we followed the path from Seathwaite Farm, crossed a footbridge over a lively beck and negotiated an unusual stile. It is in two sections, reared at an angle of about 45% on either side of huge rocks.

Our path went upwards in short zig-zags, reinforced irregularly by stones, but here and there we were on bare, angled rock – what Mr Wainwright had referred to as a "simple scramble". They were moderately hard to negotiate on a day when wetness made them slippery. The path came daringly close to Sourmilk Falls and we were entranced by the flow of white water over dark rocks.

We continued the climb on the Gillercomb route to Great Gable, moving in a misty world. A raven gave its husky, bass-baritone call. To our left – the map assured us – was Base Brown. To our right, somewhere in the mist, should be Grey Knotts, which that day was exceptionally well named.

The flagged way meandered and climbed towards the ridge, thence on to Green Gable. We saw little beyond wet rocks, wet scree and wet cairns. We stormed crags that stood like the grey walls of a fortress and we followed a line of cairns – up, up, up in the silence and mist – to the summit of Green Gable, where we had enough energy to tap the cairn as a mark of conquest.

There followed a scree descent into Windy Gap and a potentially ankle-wrack-ing climb, first over fine material, then over a ruckle of disorderly wet stones on to Great Gable. We had started not caring whether we reached the cairn on Great Gable for 11 a.m. or not. A glance at our watches and the sense of purpose shown by other walkers indicated we might be just in time to reach the poppy-fes-tooned memorial plaque at the appointed time.

The mist was thick, the air not only damp but lively, the temperature low. We slithered and clattered our way over stones until, in the mist, we made out the form of a rambler sitting on a rock eating a sandwich, and other ramblers sitting or standing around, restless, clock-watching. Yet more ramblers had gathered at the rock to which the memorial is attached. There were 40 of us, compared with the estimated 1,000 of the previous Sunday.

The voice of one of the ramblers was heard: "I think it's about 11 o'clock." It was, of course, precisely 11 o'clock. Caps were doffed, heads were bowed, and the customary two minutes' silence began. Popsie, standing on a big boulder near where I was standing, capless, with head bowed, reached out and licked my spec-tacles. The seconds ticked by. Then the voice of the unknown rambler spoke the famous lines by Binyon: "They shall not grow old, as we that are left grow old...." We all repeated the last line: "We will remember them".

The rapping of my walking stick and the occasional clink of stones marked the descent down the breast of Great Gable to Sty Head. We took pains to ensure we were on the right path and then moved cautiously beside Raven Crag and Dry Tarn. Into view, as the last tatters of mist were swept away, came Great End, its sides scored by deep gills. A rambler with a Tyneside accent said the route we had used was hardly a Stairway to Heaven but marginally better than the scramble of years ago.

Some lads had gathered at the First Aid box to have their food. We followed an ankle-aching path from Sty Head Tarn to where the path descends to the head of Borrowdale. David announced that according to Wainwright we had climbed 2,700 ft and descended 2,600 ft. The discrepancy might have had something to do with the blundering on Green Gable.

We walked – nay, marched – into Seathwaite, then called at the Scafell Hotel at Rosthwaite for cold drinks, crisps and salted peanuts. Popsie enjoyed the crisps but spat out the peanuts.

Pilgrimage 25 – Cross Fell

If you decide to reach the summit plateau of Cross Fell, highest of the Pennine fells, you would benefit from having a copy of Ordnance Survey Outdoor Leisure map No. 31, which covers the Northern Pennines and shows the route of the Pennine Way, Britain's second longest footpath, which connects Derbyshire with Scotland.

Basic Details

A pilgrim with a car should go to the small village of Knock, at the foot of the Pennines to the east of Penrith, and, using a cul-de-sac road that serves the radome establishment on Great Dun Fell, motor as far as a car park. Complete the journey to the summit of the fell on your two feet, joining the Pennine Way to walk over Little Dun Fell and then to ascend to the bare, windswept acres of Cross Fell (2,930 ft). In recent years, much of the felltop stretch has been (comfortingly) flagged with imported stone, so there is no sploshing across marshy ground.

Someone, presumably a monk, climbed to the bare, windswept high plateau of the northern Pennines and raised a cross at a point which used to be known as Fiends Fell. The cross has long since gone, but the name Cross Fell endures. It is the "attic" of the Pennines, reached by a hard slog, which means an excursion is for the hale and hardy who can use a compass in conjunction with the map and have durable clothes against the onset of grim weather.

Cross Fell has a grim reputation. In 1747, a geographer described it as "a mountain that is generally ten months bury'd in snow, and eleven in clouds", which is hardly true, though the first snow of the winter seems to settle here and its gleaming pate is therefore identifiable from a great distance. Cross Fell is noted for the violence of its winds, and especially the Helm Wind, which is brewed in a vast cauldron known as High Cup Nick.

The Helm begins when an air current from the east is cooled in its slow progress up the eastern slopes and, at the rim of the Pennines, pours down into Edenvale, some 3,000 ft below. The wind which is created rages along the East Fellside but is said not to cross the river Eden.

Pilgrim's Way

A recommended route is given above. In good weather, the vistas are breathtaking. From the summit itself, little more is seen than the area immediately around, with the sky occupying two-thirds of the view. You will have to walk around the rim for the best views. Westwards is the Eden Valley and to the north the blue hills of Scotland. The eastward prospect is of the austere dales and moors of Durham and the upper Tees.

The dotterel, one of our rarest breeding birds, has been seen on Cross Fell. Up here, too, you might observe the golden plover, the "Pennine whistler".

Pilgrimage 26 – Mr Wainwright's Vision

Our first call is at Buttermere Church where, on a window sill, there is a plaque commemorating A Wainwright, fell-wanderer, artist, writer and compiler of a notable set of Lakeland guides. Through the window, in clear weather, can be seen Hay Stacks, the fell on which he elected to have his ashes scattered. The terrain is steep and rough on the outward journey and rather better for the return. But be prepared for a rapid change of weather by having a compass as well as the map and some durable clothing.

Wainwright, the celebrated compiler of hand-written, hand-drawn guide books to the Lakeland Fells, would have been embarrassed, if not annoyed, to have been included in a book of pilgrimages. As a lad in Blackburn, with a God-fearing, chapel-going mother, he was familiar with Nonconformist worship. In adulthood, he almost prided himself on his lack of religious affiliation.

Yet when he and a cousin visited the Lake District for a holiday, and stood on Orrest Head, with a view across Windermere to the Coniston Fells, he thought he had attained heaven on earth. And so deeply did the beauty of the Lakeland Fells stir him that he found a job in the accountancy department at Kendal Town Hall and spent most of his leisure-time in Lakeland.

Wainwright was a loner in his fell-top world, lost in his own thoughts, not suffering fools gladly, speaking – Quaker style – only when the spirit moved him. In his fell-going, he travelled lightly, wearing everyday togs, with an old raincoat to turn the worst of the weather.

He had no need for a rucksack. He pocketed his pipe and tobacco, his few provisions and the camera he used to photograph the fells in detail. Later, he used them as the basis of his drawings, which were drawn immaculately using Indian ink on white card. Wainwright did not even carry a compass. He marked the Ordnance Survey maps and later copied from them in a way that would not be tolerated today without authority and payment of a fee.

His guide books were compiled (a page each evening) so that when he was old and too stiff-legged to climb the hills, he might refer to them and recall the joys of fell-wandering. (In the event, in old age his eyesight failed and he could no longer clearly see his miniscule drawings and text).

Pilgrim's Way

Buttermere is ringed by high fells. Fleetwith Pike stands guardian at the head of the lake. Hay Stacks, at 1,959 ft, is not far short of the 2,000 ft needed for mountainhood. Buttermere church clings to steep ground at the start of the pass leading over to Newlands Valley.

Ordnance Survey Outdoor Leisure 4 of the English Lakes (North Western Area) shows Buttermere, Gatesgarth Farm (with its Mountain Rescue Post in bold red lettering) and to the south Hay Stacks, the fell that is the object of our pilgrimage.

Notice the bold green hatched line of the footpath leading across the flats at the head of the lake to the upsweeping crags – Wainwright's "wall of defending crags" – rising from Warnscale Bottom. We use the Scarth Gap Pass, with a left turn in due course for Hay Stacks. When you reach the Hay Stacks plateau, you will walk through a labyrinth of rocks, knolls, tarns, cracks, crevices and coarse vegetation.

An 18th century cartographer wrote over Hay Stacks the words "here eagles build". The hill is not especially noted for its bird life. On the dry parts, heather blooms, bees drone from flower to flower and bilberries yield lustrous fruit. The tarns, in their peaty hollows, are flanked by expanses of cotton grass and sphagnum moss.

If Hay Stacks resembles Loughrigg from the point of view of the variety of features across its sprawling top, then it is also similar in being a relatively low vantage point for an arc of lofty fells. The romantic imagines the scattered tors to be haystacks in a summer meadow.

Wainwright's ashes were scattered beside Innominate Tarn, "where [he wrote] the water gently laps the gravelly shore and the heather blooms and Pillar and Gable keep unfailing watch...And if you, dear reader, should get a bit of grit in your boot as you are crossing Hay Stacks in the years to come, please treat it with respect. It might be me."

The return may be undertaken by walking beside Innominate Tarn and on to Blackbeck Tarn, across to a disused quarry, thence by high but good path descending to the starting point.

An Epilogue

Long may the Lake District remain as Wordsworth envisaged:

...a sort of national property, in which every man has a right and an interest who has an eye to perceive and a heart to enjoy.

Bibliography

Allen, Maureen – Caldbeck (1987)

Armstrong, Margaret – Thirlmere Across the Bridges to Chapel 1849-1852 (1989)

Barrand, Rev C N – A Short Guide to Martindale (1978)

Brigflatts Preparative Meeting – Brigflatts Meeting House leaflet

Burgess, John, and others – Christians in Cumbria (1982)

Eversley, Ruth – Wasdale (1981)

Farmer, David Hugh – The Oxford Dictionary of Saints (1978)

Gambles, Robert – Lake District Placenames (1980)

Hartley, John – North Cumberland, a Solway Group guide

Lefebure, Molly – Cumbrian Discovery (1977)

Lindop, Grevel – A Literary Guide to the Lake District (1993)

Mitchell, W R – The Lost Village of Mardale (1993)

Letters from the Lakes (1995)

Nicholson, Norman – Portrait of the Lakes (revised 1972)

The Lakers (1955)

Sale, Richard & Lees, Arthur – The Ancient Ways of Lakeland (1986)

Taylor, Christopher D – Portrait of Windermere (1983)

Taylor-Page, J – Contribution to Northern Earth Mysteries, Nos 44-45 (1990/91)

Trott, Stan and Freda – Return to the Lune Valley (1972)

Victoria and Albert Museum – The Discovery of the Lake District (1984)

Wallace, Doreen – English Lakeland (1940)

Walker, Freda M – A Little History and Guide to Hawkshead

Widdup, Henry L – The Story of Christianity in Cumbria (1981)

Winterburn, G H – Long Marton and its Church

Woodger, Phyllis L & Hunter, Jessie E – The High Chapel, Ravenstonedale (2nd edition, 1987)

Acknowledgements...

Photographs

Front: A Lakeland Dalesman, Countess Pillar near Brougham, Cedric Robinson and two Oversands walkers at Morecambe Bay, Quaker Meeting House at Brigflats.

Back: Walkers above Ullswater, Cross above the Plague Stone at Edenhall, Memorial to Thomas Arthur Leonard of the CHA on Catbells, a walker on the Howgill Fells.

Art supplement: Castlerigg Stone Circle 73, Long Meg 74, Walkers on Morecambe Bay (top) and Brigflatts (bottom) 75, Josephina Banner (top) and Patterdale Church (bottom) 76, Dacre Church (top) and Outhgill (bottom) 77, William Wordsworth (top) and Ninekirks (bottom) 78, Matterdale Church (top) and Wythburn (bottom) 79, Cartmel Priory 80.

Drawings

S Buckley – title page
Peter Fox – 8, 29, 32, 50, 57, 62, 69, 71, 103
E. Gower – 67
Griff – 33
E. Jeffrey – 4, 14, 20, 43, 63, 86, 89, 105, 114, 121, 124.